Winning Cover Letters for First-time Job Hunters

D1628180

Ann Sta

Winning Cover Letters for First-time Job Hunters

This first edition published in 2009
by Trotman Publishing an imprint of Crimson Publishing
Westminster House, Kew Road, Richmond, Surrey TW9 2ND

Author Ann Starkie

British Library Cataloguing in Publication Data
A catalogue record of this book is available from the British Library.

©Trotman Publishing 2009

ISBN: 978-1-84455-207-8

Typeset by RefineCatch Limited, Bungay, Suffolk

Printed and bound in the UK by TJ International Ltd, Padstow, Cornwall

Contents

About the author

Ann Stakie is a practicing Careers Adviser and runs an independent careers company. Her experience includes advice to school and college students, and recent graduates. She is a registered practitioner with the Institute of Career Guidance and her expertise has been used in national and regional guidance events, radio, and guidance publication.

Acknowledgements

I would like to thank in particular the following people and organisations for giving their time and expertise to this publication.

- ACAS
- Broadland Council Training Services – thanks to Sharon Money
- Cocoabean Recruitment – thanks to Mary Pratt, Brooke Boston and Emma Baughan
- Connexions Norfolk – thanks to Paul Wright, David Poulter and Mark Anderson
- iCeGS at the University of Derby for their research
- Institute of Career Guidance - thanks to Paul Hebron
- Virgin Money

Lastly, special thanks to all the young people whose cover letters made this publication possible.

Introduction

What will winning cover letters give you?

You may have picked up this book because you have recently left school, college or university and are applying for your first full-time job. You may be still studying and want some help with applying for work experience or work placements in the holidays. You may be a parent, concerned adult, teacher or adviser wanting to help someone you know with their job search.

Whatever your reason, *Winning Cover Letters for First-time Job Hunters* is here to help. It offers a straight talking, practical guide as to when to use cover letters, how they should be written and sent, and most importantly how to make your first contact with an employer a positive one.

Sometimes the thought of sitting down and sending a letter to an employer can seem daunting and off-putting. This book gives you tips and techniques throughout for overcoming common problems that will increase your confidence and which you can apply to all future letters and job applications.

The use of cover letters has changed in recent years and they are no longer just sent through the post but now are sent via email, to accompany emailed applications and CVs and even portfolios. Knowing what format to use and what is expected has become increasingly important. Part of this book is dedicated to showing how to send cover letters in a way that fits with the world of new technology and electronic communication.

I wanted to make this book easy to use and so have made much of it visual and have included a handy checklist and template. Throughout, examples are given of real first-time cover letters from young people, those in education and graduates. There are also quotes and feedback from real employers, recruitment agencies, work based learning providers and advice organisations who have years of experience of seeing first-time cover letters day in day out.

What difference will it make to you?

The simple answer to this is that it could be the difference to whether your CV or application gets read by an employer. The point of a winning cover letter is to 'sell' who you are and get an employer interested in what is great about you. The job market is tough and it is not always the best person who gets the interview or offered a job. It is the person who knows how to present themselves to the employer in a way that makes them say 'I want to know more.'

Winning cover letters are easier than you think and with the right technique and a little bit of know-how can become second nature. This will stand you in good stead throughout your working life.

1

Job applications – where do I start?

Are you ready to start job hunting? One of the biggest problems for first-time job hunters is to know where to look for jobs that will suit them.

Many first-time job seekers put in lots of applications but they waste all their hard effort because the applications are for jobs that are not suitable for them. They don't meet the main requirements for the job and are aiming at the wrong jobs.

In this chapter, we consider:

- what types of things to think about when looking for a job
- where to go to find possible jobs – a targeted approach
- what to look for in a job advert
- different types of applications
- the two essential rules to making your application a success.

Before you start on your job search it may help to think about the following.

| What kind of job do I want? | Do I want a short-term job or something that leads to a career/long-term prospects? What are my job needs right now? |
| What do I have to offer? | What skills, qualities, qualifications and experience do I have and what job could I use these in? |

[continued overleaf]

What level of job am I suitable for?	An apprenticeship, a traineeship, qualified or unqualified, professional, graduate, college leaver?
What kind of environments do I like to work in?	Do I like to work outside, in an office, do I thrive on pressure, working with lots of people or on my own?
What kinds of activities do I like doing?	Working with numbers, selling, serving the public, caring, administration, organising, fixing things.
Do I need to take account of any special needs I have or a disability? Do I have any medical issues that restrict me applying for certain types of work i.e. colour blindness?	Looking for employers that are flexible and positive to these needs, or may be understanding.
Where do I want to work? Where is it realistic for me to travel to on a daily basis?	How local do I need to work from my home? Can I take a job anywhere in the country?

Seeking help if you need it

If you find the sorts of questions above difficult to answer it may be that you would benefit from seeing a careers adviser or receiving some guidance as to what kind of jobs you would be suitable for. There are many guidance agencies to help you and some of these are listed in the resources section of this book.

Where to look for jobs – a targeted approach

Having a clear idea of what you want to apply for will help you to look in the right kind of places and look at the right type of adverts or vacancies. Time taken on finding this out will really save you effort and heartache in the long run.

Once you know what kind of job you are looking for this will lead you to look in specific newspapers, job search websites, professional magazines or journals, careers fairs, vacancy bulletins or targeted services that are best for *you*. Details of some good places to look are given in the resources section.

If you have qualifications or are on a course leading to professional qualifications in a certain industry, be aware of targeted magazines, journals and job websites for your industry sector. It is a good idea also to apply to be a student member of any professional organisations as these will often have their own job links and specific events like careers fairs or conferences.

In particular, if you are a young person just having left school, your local Connexions centre would be a good place to start. Most have a vacancy service advertising all apprenticeships and jobs for young people. In addition, the new Apprenticeship Vacancy Matching Service (AVMS) is available through www.apprenticeship.org.uk.

If you are at university or college, places such as the careers service or a jobs board in the place you are studying are worth looking at. Many institutions may also have a job shop where jobs are advertised, particularly those that are suitable for students.

Online job searching

There are many different websites to go to look for jobs online. If you are looking for a specific type of job – say a graduate job – you can choose to search on graduate job sites only, for example the graduate site Prospects at www.prospects.ac.uk.

If you are looking to get a job in a certain industry you could try to look up the professional body or main recruitment site for these types of jobs. These will often be national, for example for the police force or the NHS. Relevant national newspapers are also a good source, e.g. the *Guardian* for media jobs and *The Times* for law. Other job adverts can be found on particular company websites. You may be interested in that company or have heard of jobs going with that company and find you can apply directly through the company website.

Recruitment agencies

Not all jobs that are available appear in newspapers, or through adverts or online job sites. Some jobs are handled by employers through a recruitment agency. Agencies are asked by companies to advertise their jobs on their behalf for which they get a commission or fee. This means that the employer doesn't have the hassle of sifting through lots of applications, working out who to interview and can focus on its day to day business.

Recruitment agencies act on behalf of their clients or the employers who pay them and in this respect are not there to give you independent careers advice. However, often they may give you feedback on what you need to do to apply effectively through them. They may ask you to lay your application or CV out in a certain way, or follow certain recommendations and requirements. Before applying to any agency ask them for advice on their preferences.

Recruitment agencies often have areas of work they specialise in, for example administration, construction, accountancy and finance. Some specialise in senior professional roles which you would not be suitable for as a first-time job seeker. Others specialise in jobs that include temporary, part-time and full-time jobs suitable for first-time job seekers. Some agencies will want experience but this may have been gained in a voluntary or previous part-time capacity.

It is important you research which agencies are suitable for the types of jobs you are applying for. This information can often be gained from a careers service or from the library in your local area. Information about recruitment agencies can be gained from the Recruitment and Employment Confederation (REC) which is the main representative body in the UK for recruitment agencies. For further information on this try their website www.rec.uk.com.

Jobcentre Plus

This is a service provided by the government as part of the Department of Work and Pensions. Advisers at Jobcentre Plus offices in your local area can help advise you on vacancies and jobs, and are the main source of benefits if you are unemployed. If you are unemployed you will be expected to meet certain criteria, and the number of applications per week for which you must apply may sometimes be a condition of your benefits.

Jobcentre Plus advisers often have a lot of knowledge about employment within a given area and know which employers may be recruiting, and will be handling vacancies on behalf of employers. They also have specialist advisers who can help with finding employment if you are disabled or for example a carer. Information on Jobcentre Plus is available from the main national website www.jobcentreplus.gov.uk.

Networking

Many jobs may not actually be advertised so it can be useful to have good networks, or try to establish contacts within areas of work that interest you.

This can be done by volunteering or working part-time in an organisation. Often this can lead to you becoming more aware of job opportunities in that area of work. Sometimes it can lead directly to you being able to apply for a job as you will know when a position becomes vacant.

TIP

Creating a job file which lists jobs you have applied for, keeps together past applications, an updated CV and useful contacts can save hours when applying for jobs.

Job adverts

The process of application usually starts with seeing a job advert or vacancy that is advertised.

Consider the statement below.

FACT

It is estimated that between only 20–30% of all jobs are actually advertised.

You might be questioning now if looking at job adverts and filling in applications really is worthwhile. The answer is that adverts are worthwhile responding to but only if you have chosen wisely what to apply for, and ensuring that your application is the very best it can be. You have to make each application count.

It is sometimes difficult when you are a first-time job hunter to have the confidence to answer job adverts. There are many myths that exist about job adverts. Here are a few.

- All job adverts want loads of paid employment experience
- If you haven't got the right qualifications, you can't apply
- You have to fulfil all the requirements in a job advert
- All vacancies in a company have to be advertised, even if only internally

All job adverts want loads of paid employment experience

Many job adverts do specify previous experience but this doesn't have to come just from paid employment. Often experience gained in voluntary work, unpaid work looking after a family or relative, experienced gained while on a work placement or during work experience can be just as valid.

What is important is to think about all the types of experience you may have had before and the types of tasks you may have done during this experience. For example, if you have worked voluntarily in a charity shop or in the students' union you may have lots of relevant experience to offer. The skills you have obtained from this work may allow you to show the skills required by the advert, for example customer service skills, communication skills, or working as part of a team. If you are presently unemployed or a student and want to increase your skills and experience, getting voluntary work either through a local voluntary bureau or on a campus volunteer scheme is a great start.

If you haven't got the right qualifications, you can't apply

Most job adverts ask for certain skills, qualities and experience. Some may also specify certain qualifications, for example: 'We will be seeking a candidate with NVQ Level 2 in Care or equivalent.' If the advert requests certain professional qualification as essential then you must have these to apply. In the case as above where the term 'or equivalent' is used there may be some flexibility about which qualification will be accepted. As a general rule if the qualification is relevant to the post and it is roughly the same level then it will be considered.

You have to fulfil all the requirements in a job advert

In some job adverts the employer may specify that a certain qualification, skills, qualities or experience is desirable. This doesn't mean you must have it to apply. For example an advert for an administrator may well say that comprehensive knowledge of Excel and Word are essential but experience of Sage (an accounts package) is desirable. It is also important to note that they do not ask for a qualification in Excel and Word but comprehensive knowledge. This knowledge could have come from unpaid experience or from knowledge acquired as part of a course.

All vacancies in a company have to be advertised, even if only internally

This is quite a common myth. There is an assumption often that companies have to advertise vacancies at least to present employees even if they don't advertise externally. This is not true, companies do not have to advertise a vacancy but many do in order to ensure that they are not being discriminatory.

Don't let myths or pre-conceived ideas put you off applying for a job vacancy or advert. If you don't apply you definitely won't know if you are good enough. Each application is a chance to get better.

A note about equality of opportunity

There are many different laws governing how and what companies put into an advert. Equal opportunities legislation makes it illegal for an advert to directly or indirectly discriminate in terms of age, sex, race, disability, sexual orientation, nationality or religion. There are exceptions however where a 'genuine occupational requirement' can be shown by the employer. One example of this would be the requirement of a woman to work in a women's refuge.

Similar legal requirements exist on the selection of candidates by application, interviews and selection tests. The law around employment and selection is very complex and any issues with this should be referred to an appropriate agency such as the Citizens Advice Bureau or ACAS, details of which are given in the resources section at the back of this book.

Some employers have gone through certain quality controls and have gained awards showing they are a good employer to work for. It is worth looking out for the these types of awards such as Investors in People, or Positive About Disabled People as these employers may be more receptive and more likely to offer support for all staff.

Working out what is required in a job advert

The best way of working out what really is required by an employer for a certain position is to look at the detail in the job advert.

Consider this job advert.

MEDICAL DATA HANDLING OFFICER

Salary (scale 2–3): £9,500–£10,342
37 hours per week, Monday–Friday

Job Ref: 5071/A/191

You will be required to input data into the Medical Information System (MIS). The post is working 37 hours a week, Monday to Friday. A working knowledge of MIS is an advantage but full training will be given. Attention to detail and accuracy is essential. General secretarial duties may be required.

For an informal discussion about the post please contact Miss Sarah Fax on: (09431) 726439. The General Trust is a Positive About Disabled People employer.

To apply: Further details and an application form can be found on the website following the vacancy link on the home page www.thegeneraltrust.org.uk. Please apply by letter of application, enclosing a current CV and application form quoting the reference. Return by email to J.Joans@emailgeneraltrust.com.

Key elements of a job advert are:

The job title. In this advert the job title is fairly self explanatory but in some job adverts the job title can either be misleading or just baffling. Some industries have their own 'speak' so reading the job description and specification for any job is vital. Otherwise your idea of what a 'Project Plus Co-ordinator' is, might be sadly at odds with that of the employer.

The pay. This is always a real motivating factor but it mustn't be the only one. Choosing jobs on salary alone is likely to be unsuccessful. Remember, you have to be worth the pay on offer. If the pay seems to be too good to be true, it probably is. Consider if there is a pay scale which would allow you earn more as you gain experience.

The hours. This is worth reading carefully especially if issues of childcare or types of working pattern are important to you. Working hours of 37 hours full-time is typical but some jobs may require more. If you are under 18 there are certain legal restrictions on the hours you can work. Seek advice if necessary from one of the young person agencies listed in the resource section.

The job reference. Any job application must have the right reference number attached to it if there is one. If you don't put this on, your application may not even get processed.

Job description. The main tasks of the job are described along with any experience required. In this case experience of a certain programme is desirable but not made essential so you can apply without it.

Specific requirements. Essential and desirable: in this advert the job requirements are straightforward. No specific qualifications are required as training is given for the database system but obviously in an application for this job the applicant would stress any IT knowledge or qualifications they had.

The overall message. The message in this advert is that accuracy and attention to detail is essential and this may well be tested at interview stage for this type of job, say for example with a data checking task. Making any kind of mistake on the application form or in your cover letter or CV will therefore not go down well. Checking all parts of your application it vital.

Desirable qualities. Being flexible may also be important as other duties may be required. Also thinking about where the job is, it is likely that the data will be sensitive and confidential therefore a mature attitude and being aware of confidentiality of patient data would be important. Thinking from the employer's point of view can help pick up these kinds of wider issues. Try to picture the kind of person the employer would like.

Equal opportunities. This is a good job for someone with a disability to apply for because the employer has made a conscious effort to mention they have the Positive About Disabled People mark. Generally it shows the employer is likely to be supportive.

How to apply. In this case the hospital wants you to apply through their website. You would need to gather the necessary information, download the application form and then send the cover letter, application form and CV back to them by email. It is vital in any job application that you apply in exactly the way they have asked you to do so. Reading instructions is central to success.

A good way of working out what an employer wants is to imagine yourself writing the advert – what comes across as the strongest message, what criteria are essential? What picture do you have of the ideal candidate?

Different types of applications

There are different types of applications that you may come across, as the following examples show.

- An employer/agency may request you fill in an application form. This may be requested to be sent by post, email or filled in online.
- An employer/agency may request you to send an updated CV to them by either post or by email.
- Some employers or agencies may request an initial phone contact or later a phone interview.
- Other applications may be made up of an application form but followed by many different stages including interview, psychometric tests and even physical tests.

Many employers may state they also wish you to send a cover letter with an application form or would expect a cover letter as a matter of course, for example when sending a CV. This kind of etiquette is covered later in specific chapters of this book.

Online applications

Some applications are now processed entirely online. An online application is where an employer requires the applicant to apply through their website.

It is different from downloading an application and then sending it via email or by post. The form may be quite specific to the requirements of a particular employer and also it may be timed. This means if you don't complete a certain section in time you have to start the whole process again.

These types of applications are increasingly common and quite tricky because they give you limited time and involve reading on a screen, therefore making errors is much more likely.

If you are lucky there may be a chance to download the form or you may be given an email option. This means that you can print off the form first and effectively fill it in before doing it for real online. If this option exists definitely do it, as this will make your online application much more accurate.

If this isn't an option and you are forced to do an online application with no download, then if you can, save as you go along and try to read the sections out loud to help limit very obvious errors. Also have a dictionary handy.

Don't send it until you are happy with it and have checked the completed version. Even if this means going in and out several times. Print off the final version or keep a written copy so you know what you have written.

Making sure your application succeeds

Whatever the type of application, there are two essential rules that hold true which will determine if your application succeeds or fails.

RULE 1

Follow the instructions exactly

This means that you not only have to look carefully at the advert but also means reading and following all the instructions given on how to fill out the application, what the employer wants and the way they want the information.

RULE 2

Target all the information about yourself to the job

For any application to succeed you must read and understand the main functions of the job and what the employer is looking for from an applicant. You must then make sure you are this applicant by matching yourself to those requirements.

Quiz

What have you learnt about applications?

1   One of the most common mistakes first-time job hunters make when looking for jobs is:
   a) to choose jobs that are not suitable for them
   b) to choose jobs that pay too little
   c) to choose jobs for which there is too much competition.

2   The best way to start thinking about possible jobs is:
   a) to think about how much money you want to earn
   b) to think about what you like doing and are good at
   c) to ask a friend about what you should do.

3   One of the most common errors made when first-time job hunters apply for a job is:
    a)   they give too much information about themselves
    b)   they do not give enough information about themselves
    c)   they do not make the information about themselves relevant to the job.

4   The percentage of jobs actually advertised is:
    a)   50–60%
    b)   20–30%
    c)   10%

5   To successfully apply for a job you have to:
    a)   meet all the criteria for the job
    b)   meet all the desirable criteria for the job
    c)   meet all the essential criteria for the job.

6   The key factor to ensure your application succeeds is:
    a)   to make sure you are very thorough
    b)   to make sure you say how great the employer is
    c)   to make sure you read and follow the instructions exactly.

Answers

1   a
2   b
3   c
4   b
5   c
6   c

2

What is a cover letter? What is it for?

By the end of this chapter you will be clear about:

- the purpose behind the cover letter
- what different formats and styles a cover letter can come in
- what a cover letter should not be

You might be thinking why do I even need to know about cover letters? A cover letter is just something that goes with an application or CV and is not really that important. Does anyone even use cover letters anymore now many applications are done by email or online?

The image of a cover letter is understated and often confused. Far from being just an addition to your application or CV, a cover letter is in fact an extremely important part of the application process. This is because it is the first thing an employer sees. If you don't make a good first impression with the cover letter you have sent, then no matter how good your CV or application, you just won't get any further. Consider this statement below.

> **FACT**
> On average employers spend less than 60 seconds on any individual application when it first reaches them.

If you want your application to be put on the pile for further consideration then the cover letter you send has to create a great first impression.

The other main reason that a cover letter is so important is because it is your first chance to express who you are and what you have to offer to an employer. It is a way of showing someone you don't know something personal about you. A cover letter through its tone and the words used creates an impression to the employer of you as an individual. CVs and applications are quite prescriptive and don't offer this kind of first impression.

One employer explained:

> 'We get letters all the time here asking for jobs and work experience. What I am really looking for is the one where their enthusiasm to be a hairdresser just leaps off the page. If I can't feel that, then I don't take that application any further.'

What is a cover letter?

When you see an advert for a job or you want to write to an employer, you are often asked to write a cover letter. Knowing exactly what a cover letter is and what should go into one is however quite a mystery. This is because there is not one type of cover letter. What goes into the letter depends what you are intending on using it for. However, there are some common aspects about all cover letters that hold true. A cover letter is:

- a business letter – this means it has to look professional
- a letter with a particular purpose – responding to a vacancy or following up an enquiry
- a letter which creates a favourable impression – the person receiving it wants to know more/respond
- a letter prompting action – it needs to say, 'If you are interested, then look at my CV or application'.

A cover letter is not:

- a begging letter – please give me a job I am desperate
- a shortened version of your CV – rewording parts of your CV into a letter
- a biography of your life – an opportunity to say everything about you
- a letter of complaint or opinion – a chance to put the world right.

What formats can cover letters come in?

Cover letters can differ depending on how you have found out about the job you are applying for. Maybe you saw a job advert and so you have clear instructions as to who to send your letter to and the exact role you are applying for. But you may be sending a letter with your CV on the off chance that there is a vacancy with a company or for the company to bear you in mind as soon as a vacancy comes up.

Cover letters can be:

- letters of application – these are letters that respond to a vacancy or advert
- letters of interest – these are letters that express your interest in a vacancy or job advert
- speculative letters/speculative applications – these are letters that you write asking an organisation for an opportunity when it is not advertised

What is the purpose of a cover letter?

Consider which of these statements below are true or false.

Quick Quiz

1   A cover letter is used to introduce you to an employer or another individual.   T/F

2   A cover letter is used to persuade an employer to give you a job.   T/F

3   A cover letter is used to get you noticed quickly and by as many employers as possible.   T/F

4   A cover letter is used to accompany a CV or application form.   T/F

5 A cover letter is used to ask someone you know to help you find a job. T/F

6 A cover letter is used to reply to a job offer. T/F

7 A cover letter is used to apply for work experience. T/F

8 A cover letter is used to reply to specific job adverts or vacancies. T/F

Answers

1. A cover letter is used to introduce you to an employer or another individual.

True: A cover letter is a professional way to introduce yourself to an employer or professional contact. A cover letter should be addressed to a named in-dividual within an organisation along with their title. You should explain your reason for writing, and draw out relevant aspects about yourself.

2. A cover letter is used to persuade an employer to give you a job.

False: This is not the primary purpose of a cover letter although in most cases it may be the eventual aim. A cover letter is written to get an employer to look at your CV, application form or to consider you for interview. It cannot by itself get you a job. It is merely the first part of getting the employer to read your CV or application or take you to the next stage. Remembering this should stop you from writing a letter that tries to be all things, and actually achieves nothing.

3. A cover letter is used to get you noticed quickly and by as many employers as possible.

False: Cover letters are used sometimes to write to lots of employers asking for opportunities that may not be advertised. The generic approach, where the letter is addressed Dear Sir/Madam and the same cover letter is sent round to multiple employers, is not good practice or likely to succeed. Letters like this are considered of little or no value to an employer. They are not personal, and are likely to be put straight in the bin.

4. A cover letter is used to accompany a CV or application form.

True: A cover letter is usually read first by the employer and then the accompaning CV or application form. A cover letter always accompanies a CV and may accompany an application depending on what is directed by the employer. This means reading the advert or job application carefully to see what is required.

5. A cover letter is used to ask someone you know to help you find a job.

False: This approach is doomed to failure. The recipient is often extremely embarrassed and is put in an awkward position. The type of letter which uses your network of friends and colleagues is better used as a way of re-establishing contact or finding out information. When a cover letter is used to ask for information or for an informal meeting only the letter fits a purpose which is far more productive and likely to succeed.

6. A cover letter is used to reply to a job offer.

True: A cover letter can be used to reply to a job offer, to accept or reject one. It can also be used to negotiate terms and conditions of starting a job. It may be used also to refer to references you have gathered following an interview. Although you may not be introducing yourself, you still have to express yourself favourably and professionally in this type of letter.

7. A cover letter is used to apply for work experience.

True: A cover letter is often used to gain unpaid work experience or voluntary work. This is particularly relevant when you may have just left school or university and you want to gain some real life experience in an employment setting. A letter like this is also used often for work experience in Years 10 and 11 at school. This type of letter could potentially lead to a full-time position so should be as professional as one responding to a job vacancy.

8. **A cover letter is used to reply to specific job adverts or vacancies.**

True: This is a common use of a cover letter. Sometimes job advertisements may ask for a cover letter and no CV. These types of advert do still exist although they are considered by some to be old fashioned.

Sometimes the advert may request that the letter is handwritten. This is something to be aware of. If it doesn't state the letter has to be handwritten then it will be acceptable in most cases to word process the letter. If it does request handwritten, then you must do the letter in your own handwriting. If you are really not sure, then ring up the contact on the advert and ask.

A cover letter is very important because it is the first chance you have to show who you are to an employer. It has to be a professional document and clear in its purpose. It must be written to a particular individual and the information in it made relevant to that individual and organisation.

3

How to write your cover letter

You may have often heard the expression, 'It is not what you do it is the way that you do it.' This is a useful way of thinking about how to write a cover letter.

This chapter will offer advice on:

- making sure you choose the right cover letter for the job you're applying for
- the five key elements to remember when writing your cover letter
- how to ensure your grammar and punctuation is perfect.

Although two letters may have similar content, the way in which they are laid out, formatted, the style used, the words and phrases chosen and the way it is sent all can make a huge difference to how the cover letter or cover email is received. This can make the difference between success and rejection.

There are lots of different types of cover letter; traditional, emailed, hand written and speculative to name but a few.

Before you even think about writing a cover letter you need to think through three things.

1 What do I want the end result of the letter to be? i.e. To get work experience, to get the employer to read my CV.
2 What kind of impression do I want to give of myself to the employer? e.g. Enthusiastic, willing to learn, first class graduate, someone who goes the extra mile.

3   Where am I pitching myself – what am I aiming for? Am I applying for a job which needs lots of qualifications or experience I don't have? Am I applying for jobs that don't interest me or are beneath my ability? Try to be realistic but enthusiastic.

These three points will help you start to form your cover letter. The next part is about knowing some basic writing skills to make your letter. As one employer said:

> 'I am amazed by how many applicants don't know the basics. They don't know how to put a letter together, use the right grammar or sign off their letters correctly. Maybe these sorts of skills are not taught anymore. Unfortunately it often means they miss out.'

Choosing the right type of cover letter

So how do you go about choosing what type of cover letter to use? There are three essential things to think about.

1   Who am I writing to?
2   Why am I writing?
3   What has the employer asked for/what is their preference?

Choosing the type of cover letter to send depends on what the company has asked for or what type of company it is. In some cases this is straightforward, such as when it is a response to an advert or the employer has told you what they want.

In the case of a speculative cover letter you may not have had any previous contact with the organisation or employer. It is therefore vital to do some background research either on the web or by asking for a company brochure.

TIP If in doubt ask. If you wish to write a letter without any previous contact with an employer it is always a good idea to ring and ask who would be the best person to send your letter to and how they would like it sent. This will also save you wasting your time and effort with companies that don't accept any kind of speculative application. Some tips for how to make this kind of phone call are given in Chapter 4.

Writing a speculative cover letter

A speculative letter is a letter written to an employer on the off-chance they may have a vacancy that is suitable or one coming up shortly in the future. In this sense it is written blind as there is no advert or vacancy to respond to. However, careful research beforehand of the company can ensure that the letter comes across as well targeted and prepared.

Below is an example of a speculative letter.

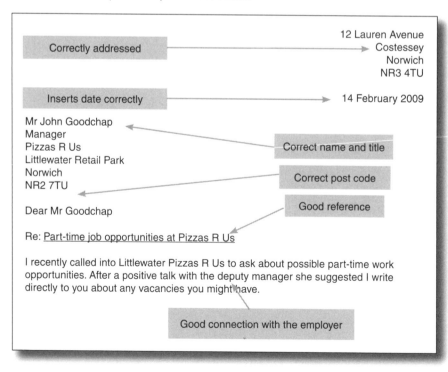

I am presently a student at a local college studying A levels and am looking to gain some part-time work in the evenings and weekends to help me fund my present and future studying.

> Explains well what he can offer

I have previous experience of part-time work from a paper round I undertook for two years while at school and I helped at a summer camp last year at Costessey Leisure Centre. This involved talking with the general public and taking responsibility for young children, including children with dietary problems.

> Makes his experience relevant

I would particularly like to work at the Littlewater location as I am local and the retail park is only a few minutes drive from my home. I have a clean driving licence and access to a car. I am free most days by 4p.m. and every weekend.

> Shows employer advantage on being so close

I have attached my CV for your consideration. If you wish to contact me, either during lunch at 12:30–1:30 or after 4p.m. is probably the easiest time as I am not in classes then. My mobile number is 0776234762.

Yours sincerely,

Jamie Student

> Tells the employer when he can get hold of him

Enclosed × 1

Jamie has really helped the employer by researching first that there are vacancies going before sending the letter. He has also included when he is available and what he can offer. This shows consideration for the employer and makes it easy for them to work out if they can offer Jamie anything straight away.

Jamie has pointed out his previous experience and although not in fast food, he has made it relevant to the role at Pizzas R Us by pointing out it includes

TIP

Think about the type of employer you are applying to and what demands they may have on their time. If you are applying for work experience placement or voluntary work try to find out what times would suit them or what they might be able to offer that fits in with you and *them*. This is particularly important in speculative cover letters.

working with the public and understanding dietary needs. He also has attached his CV and made a point of telling the employer when he can easily be contacted. This again helps the employer save time knowing when he will be able to speak to Jamie directly.

Handwritten letters

Handwritten letters are now increasingly uncommon but they still are preferred by some employers. Some employers may also analyse the handwriting for indicators of personality for example. These companies are often looking for management level positions and employ an experienced and respected graphologist to undertake the analysis. This is less common in the UK but more widely used in Europe. The companies include investment, legal, recruitment, vehicle and jewellery companies.

Where an employer specifically states they want a handwritten cover letter then this should be followed. If nothing is stated then it is fair to assume it can be typed. The basic rule is that handwritten letters should be well laid out, with defined paragraphs. They should be neat and easy to read.

It may be that a handwritten letter must be written out several times to get them neat enough. It should not contain mistakes as in the case below.

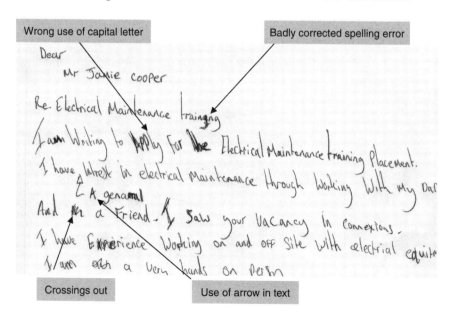

Typed emails or cover letters

Fonts

Two fonts which are most regularly used for typing and emailing cover letters are Arial or Times New Roman. These two fonts are the most used as they are clear to read and look professional. Also it is not useful to try to type a letter in a font that looks like it is handwritten, such as Lucinda Handwriting. Always use the same font throughout.

Font size should be no smaller than 10 and the most commonly used size is 12. You should not alter your font size through the letter, i.e. for headings, as this only looks confusing.

Personal style

Writing a cover letter on good quality A4 paper is straightforward. However, with emails the ability to adapt the background wallpaper of your email or send your signature in fun loving style/font may not be to your advantage.

Often if you have adapted the background of your email through tools and options you can easily forget that this may not be appropriate for your job hunting emails. If you have two email accounts, one for job hunting and one for friends, this allows you to keep your funky styles for your friends while coming across as professional and serious to potential employers. This also goes for email addresses too.

> **TIP** Don't forget the envelope. There is little point in sending an immaculate letter in an envelope with a coffee stain on it. It might not even get opened!

Five key elements to remember

To get a cover letter right you have to go back to basics. It is a bit like laying good foundations before building a house. There are five key areas when creating a cover letter. These are:

1   presentation
2   format and style
3   tone
4   relevancy
5   accuracy

Presentation

The presentation of the letter is crucial. If you are doing a formal traditional letter then it must come across like a business letter. It must be presented on good quality white A4 paper if it is to be printed or written. If sent by email it must be presented in the proper fashion to the recipient. One recruiter made the following statement.

> 'I have got a letter and CV printed on multicoloured paper. Honestly I have. Not only was it printed on coloured paper but each heading in the letter and the CV was in a different colour. You just can't take someone who does that seriously, can you?'

There are some basic rules to ensure that the presentation of your cover letter is spot on.

These are:

- it must be fit for purpose
- it must fit the preference of the employer
- it should be highly presentable in looks, paper quality and type
- it must be easy to understand and read
- it must tell the truth and any claims must be able to be supported
- it must never contain crossings out or corrective features like arrows
- it shouldn't go over one side of A4
- it should not just repeat information from your CV
- it should not use clichés or offensive words/opinions
- it must not contain negative words or expressions.

Format and style

The format of a cover letter means the type of letter you are going to send and how it is laid out. There are two main formats for a cover letter.

1   You are applying for a job vacancy or an advert.
2   You are making a speculative application or asking for something which has not been advertised.

The style of a cover letter is the way in which it is written. It includes things like the font size and font choice, choosing whether to hand write or type a letter.

Some companies in the legal profession still request handwritten letters, which are used to apply for positions as solicitors. Sometimes handwritten letters are also requested for certain secretarial positions, usually personal assistant vacancies where an employer has a preference for a more traditional style application. Also handwritten letters may be used by employers where handwriting will be used in the job, for example a florist.

Tone

Have you ever had a conversation with someone and although the words sound right their general tone of voice tells you that something is not? This can occur with telephone calls and also with cover letters. Picking up these 'cues' in everyday life is often referred to as emotional intelligence. It is easy when someone is in front of you as you can see what is happening, but with a letter you just have what you are reading.

Creating a favourable impression is all about getting the *tone of the letter right*. Your natural tone may be quick, chirpy and funny. You might be known as the class clown or the scatty one. Your friends and family will understand this because they know you well. An employer however, coming across you for the first time, will not.

Being aware of how you come across is very important. Adapting the tone of a letter or conversation so that it fits the expectations of the employer is essential if you are to succeed.

Look at this example written to a local IT employer.

> 'I have more than enough experience to fulfil this role having worked at GCS in my last placement at University. I would class myself as one of the top IT graduates in my year and would expect to start at middle management level.'

Did you pick up the tone from this letter? Would you employ this person or even want to spend any time with them? The writer comes across as arrogant. This graduate obviously feels they have more experience and skills than the employer, so this type of tone is one likely to alienate the employer immediately.

Relevancy

Making your letter relevant to the employer is one of the most essential parts to a successful cover letter. It is often missed and it can make a big difference to an employer.

An employer wants to know that you have the skills, experience and interest in their line of work that can make a *difference to them*. They don't want to know if you have the most qualifications or if you have travelled round the world just for the sake of it. They want to know how this might help them.

Look at the two examples below.

EXAMPLE 1

I have just recently finished a course in Travel and Tourism. I want to become a travel agent. I feel that I have loads of experience and skills to offer an employer. I am really reliable and honest and enjoy travelling.

In Example 1 the applicant has said what they have done and hints at experience but does not explain what this means for the employer. They also mention they like travelling but give no details about why this is relevant to the kind of work they will be doing. It gives the employer the feeling that the applicant thinks working in a travel agency is all about fun and travel and not about selling or retail.

EXAMPLE 2

I have recently completed an Advanced level course in Travel and Tourism. This has enabled me to understand customer service, UK and European travel destinations, retail and business, and travel operations.

As part of the course we undertook a two week placement in a local travel agency. I learnt about local travel options and the local area as well as more distant destinations.

This placement helped me gain skills in communicating with the public, problem solving, and using my initiative. I feel that at First For Travel I would be able to utilise these skills from the first day of training.

In Example 2 the applicant has said directly how their previous course and experience can make them useful to the employer. They have taken time to mention what they have learnt and how this may directly apply to this traineeship.

Accuracy

The four main villains to accuracy are:

1. poor spelling
2. incorrect use of grammar
2. punctuation
4. confusable words

Spelling

The only way to get spellings right is to look them up in a dictionary. The preferred dictionary for English spellings is the *Oxford English Dictionary* and copies of this are available in libraries and many bookshops. If you are unsure it is better to check spellings with a dictionary as many spell checkers use American spellings.

If English is your second or third language then using the correct phrases can also be difficult. Books such as the *Oxford Thesaurus* may help you choose alternative words. For further details on guides and websites see the resources section at the back of this book.

Useful grammar tips

Below is a quick and simple explanation of some key grammatical terms.

Term	What it means	Example
First Person	Writing 'I' not 'We' or 'Them'	'I am writing to you with regard to the vacancy I saw in *The Echo* last Thursday for a sales assistant.' Cover letters are written in the first person.
Tenses	Past, present, future	It is important to make sure that if you are writing in the present tense, for example 'I am', that the rest of the words in that sentence are in the same tense. For example if you start in the past tense 'I have recently **finished** a degree in Music Technology and **gained** an upper second degree,' both verbs 'gained' and 'finished' are past tense.
Nouns	Proper nouns and common nouns	Proper nouns have capitals as they refer to a specific person, name, place or thing. For example; The University of East Anglia. Common nouns refer to general things, people, or places. For example, 'students from most universities prefer to live in rented accommodation'. Here there is no specific university named but just generally universities. **This is a common mistake so look out next time you type a general noun.**
Pronouns	Refers to a previously identified noun	For example, 'They said that it was better to take part in the race than to win it.' This refers to a previous identification of 'They', i.e. students from Cambridge. In this case the 'They' refers to Cambridge students.

[continued]

Term	What it means	Example
Verbs	Doing words	These are known as 'doing' words, i.e. running, working, playing. The tense defines the time of the action, for example, 'I am performing well at school' (present), as opposed to 'I performed well at school' (past).
Active Verbs		Active verbs can be useful in a letter as they can give the letter a positive feel. Use of active verbs or power words are helpful in making you sound good, for example, 'I was responsible for a team of eight sales staff' rather than 'I worked with a team of sales staff.' Of course you have to tell the truth.
Adjectives	Describing words	'I was happy to receive the award for best employee of the year.' This describes the mood of the award winner. This can add tone to your letter.
Writing concise sentences	Short and to the point	Writing concise sentences means paying attention to how many words go into one sentence. This means thinking of a short way to say the same thing. For example, 'I am a person who is considered honest' would become 'I am an honest person.' It is a good idea to write concise sentences.
Qualifier	Moderators or words that accentuate	These are words that moderate or qualify another word, for example, 'I was slightly disappointed not to pass all my GCSEs'. Qualifiers can often downgrade a phrase so it is best to keep these to a minimum unless using them in a positive way, i.e. 'I was extremely excited.'
Plurals	More than one	When making nouns plural you often add s or es, for example students, patients. Some words have a plural form, for example children is the plural form of child.
Abbreviations	Shortened words	Not all abbreviations are bad. Many abbreviations are necessary, for example Dr, UK. These types of abbreviations are expected. However, abbreviating common words as you might in a text is not acceptable in cover letters. For example U, R, or 4.

An excellent reference guide is the *Oxford Dictionary to English Grammar* which explains different aspects of grammar. Also there are various online guides to grammar to help you check grammatical mistakes, and which are mentioned in the resources section.

Punctuation – common errors

- **Full stops and capital letters.** The use of full stops and capital letters is often not followed correctly. Common errors include forgetting to put full stops at the end of sentences or putting capital letters for words or nouns that don't need them.
- **Commas.** Commas are used when there is need for sentences to be broken up. They can also be used in the case of long sentences for a breathing space. Commas are often overused. Often this happens where sentences are too long and should be shortened.
- **Colons and semi-colons.** Colons and semi-colons are often mixed up. Colons often follow the words 'for example'. Colons tell the reader to pause and have a longer pause than semi-colons. Semi-colons are often used in sentences to make a break that is longer than a comma, e.g. 'Most of our students have achieved excellent results; they deserve this as they worked hard for their grades'.
- **Apostrophes.** A classic mistake is putting an apostrophe where it isn't needed. The most commonly seen mistake in cover letters is putting GCSE's rather than the correct GCSEs. Apostrophes are used to show something belongs to someone or something (e.g. Anne's camera), or to show missing letters (e.g. don't leave your bag behind).
- **Hyphens.** These are used to join words together and also to split words up. The most common mistake with these is putting too many hyphens in a letter.
- **Dashes and brackets.** These are used to insert information into text or dates i.e. J. Jacob (1986). Common mistakes include overuse of dashes, placing them in the wrong place and putting brackets where they are not needed.

Confusable words

Confusable words are words that sound or look like other words but actually have a different meaning. These often give away to an employer that you don't actually know what a word means or that your use of English is not that good.

It is always worth checking in a dictionary to make sure that you have got the right word for what you mean to say. Some typical examples of confusable words are given below:

Word	Meaning	Confusable word	Meaning
accept	take as yes, take as true	except	not including
advice	opinion given	advise	to give advice or opinion
affect	pretend to have or feel or be	effect	change produced by an action or cause
by	near, beside	buy	obtained in exchange for money
insure	protect by insurance	ensure	make safe or certain
passed	move onward	past	belonging to the time before the present
quiet	with little or no sound	quite	completely, somewhat, really
your	belonging to you	you're	you are

4

What information goes into a cover letter?

This chapter will look at the three fundamental elements to remember when deciding what to put into your cover letter.

- **Who are you writing to?** Remember that professional letter templates require certain information (your address, the employer's address etc.) Other letters such as an email cover letter will require you to write exactly what attachments you are sending with the email in case they do not arrive. These technical elements are important when creating your cover letter because attention to these details creates a good first impression.
- **What can you offer an employer and why you are interested in them?** You will need to tell them your skills, personal qualities, past experience and interests clearly. You will also need to show your heart is in it, through your interest in the knowledge of the company and product.
- **Meeting the requirements of the employer.** If you are applying to a job advert you need to bring out in your letter all the main points the advert asks for. You must show you have read the advert carefully and you have fitted the information in your letter around what has been asked for in the job advert.

A professional winning cover letter should contain seven main parts. A handy template and checklist can be found on pp 42-3.

A template cover letter

Now let's put all this information together into a template for a cover letter you would send through the post or email as an attachment.

Your address and postcode
Your telephone no
Your email address

Date of writing

Addressee i.e. Mr J Jones
Their job title i.e. Human Resources Manager
The Company
The Street
The County
Postcode (in full) – (all these details should be available on a company website)

Dear xxxx (input name of addressee) i.e. *Mr Jones*
Re: put vacancy number or reason you are writing in here: i.e. *Customer Service Vacancies*

Paragraph 1
This should introduce you to an employer in a relevant way. You should say why you are writing. Try to find a 'hook'. This is something that refers to a mutual previous contact, meeting or telephone conversation. Make the opening strong and positive.
I was very pleased to meet you at the careers fair at the Eastern Forum last Thursday. I was impressed with the opportunities in customer care you offered and the staff training programme.

Paragraph 2
Explain in this paragraph what you can offer in relation to the jobs in terms of your previous skills, experience/interests, qualities and qualifications. Explain what makes you right for this vacancy or company.
I have recently completed an NVQ level 2 in Retail. As part of this I have worked part-time in a local shoe retailer for the last year. My training included all aspects of customer care, sales and legal matters such as the Trade Descriptions Act. I have excellent communication skills, and received top marks on my course for my sales approach. I am polite, well presented and able to work calmly under pressure.

Paragraph 3
Explain why you are interested in this company. Use one or two pieces of company knowledge and say how this fits your plans/your strengths/interests.
I am particularly interested in working for the Jacob Group as I know that it has an excellent local and national reputation for quality products and consumer service. I feel that it would help me further my career in retail customer service.

Final paragraph
Use a positive closing statement. Say what you want to happen next.
I attach my Curriculum Vitae for your consideration of any vacancies at this time. I look forward to hearing from you shortly.

Sign off your letter correctly
Yours sincerely (if you have started with Mr, Ms or Mrs)

Allow 4–6 spaces ideally
Sarah Smart Insert you name here
Any attachments or enclosures *i.e. Enc* × *1 or Attach: CV*

The cover letter checklist

You can use this form to make sure you have got all the different parts of a letter covered correctly.

Part 1 – contact information

Your name, address and postcode ☐
Your telephone and email ☐
Date of letter (left hand side) ☐
The person's name you are addressing ☐
Their title ☐
The name of the company ☐
The first line of the company address ☐
The second line of the company address ☐
The county ☐
The postcode ☐

Part 2 – opening salutation and reference of the job

The person's name you are addressing after Dear ☐
Any vacancy number or job title ☐

Part 3 – the first paragraph

Explain why you are writing ☐
Include a hook and/or wow factor ☐

Part 4 – the second paragraph

Explain what you can offer, in relation to the job ☐

Explain what makes *you* right for the position ☐

Part 5 – the third paragraph

Explain why you are interested in this company ☐

Use one or two pieces of company knowledge and say how

this fits your plans/your strengths/interests ☐

Part 6 – the final paragraph

Use a positive closing statement ☐

Say what you want to happen next ☐

Part 7 – the final salutation and enclosure details

Sign off 'Yours sincerely' (provided you used a name) ☐

Sign the letter and put details of enclosures ☐

Remember when using templates or checklists these are only a guide and you need to check and make your application fit what you have been asked to do.

Researching the company – a little knowledge goes a long way

This is one of the most important parts of the cover letter. Often this is forgotten or skipped but is actually the part of the letter which grabs the employer's attention. Showing a level of knowledge you have about a company can really make a difference to creating a good impression in your cover letter.

So how do you research a company you are interested in? The best way is to look on the internet, particularly if the company has a website. If the company is local you could even pop in to get a brochure or ring and ask for a brochure to be sent. You can also search local press websites for recent articles mentioning the company.

What to look for

You are looking to see what the company's main areas of business are, who their clients might be and the type of person they employ. Look at the logo and style of the company website or brochure. Is it traditional, conservative, out of the box, or radical? This will give you not only important information to include in the third paragraph about the company but a feel as to how the letter should be presented.

Look to see what the company is planning for the future. This information can be used to inform your cover letter and also the interview you are going to get.

The seven parts explained

Part 1 – contact and initial information

One of the first things you will put on your cover letter if you are sending it by post is your address. All addresses should be given in full. Your address is given on the right side of the letter above that of the employers, which is given on the left side. All addresses should have postcodes. It is customary also to write the date above the employers address in full again i.e. 1 July 2009.

Part 2 – opening greeting and reference

The greeting goes after the address of the employer or person you are writing to.

This is one of the areas of writing a letter which can be difficult to remember. If you start your letter Dear Mr Jones or use a name i.e. Dear Carol, then you finish the letter with the ending of Yours sincerely. The Y of yours is always capital and s is always small. If you however start your letter Dear Sir/or Madam then you would end your letter with Yours faithfully. Again the Y is capital and the f is small.

These endings are part of a basic formal etiquette of letter writing. These endings would also be applied to a full cover letter email.

One easy way to remember which ending goes with which greeting is to never put two 'S' words together. That way you will remember if it is Dear Sir/Madam it is always Yours faithfully.

Title for the letter or subject

In a written letter this is put in the line beneath the greeting. This is often referred to as Re, which means with reference to. After this you put in the job reference number or a few words describing what you are writing about. The R is always a capital and e is always lower text. For example:

Dear Mrs Jones
Re: Work experience

or

Dear Mr Davis
Re: Job reference 7283 Trainee Carpenter

Putting a clear subject is very important as it tells the reader the main focus for your letter. If there is more than one job going it is important to make it clear which one you are writing about.

Part 3 – the first paragraph

In the first section of the letter you are introducing yourself to the employer for the first time. It is helpful if you can find something you and the employer have in common or will particularly grab the employer's attention. This is sometimes called a 'hook'. If you are applying for a job you need to say what it is about this job that interests you.

Part 4 – the second paragraph

This is where you state what you have to offer e.g. skills, qualities, experience and interests in relation to the job/company.

Here is where you explain what you can offer in relation to the requirements of the position (this means you must have read the advert and/or job details very carefully).

Part 5 – the third paragraph

Here you explain your interest in the employer, why you want to work for them particularly, and why the company and what they do interests you.

Part 6 – the final paragraph

This is the closing statement. End on a positive note and state what you would like the employer to do next. For example: 'I look forward to hearing from you shortly'; 'I attach my CV for your consideration.'

Part 7 – the closing salutation

This is where you put your signature and the number of enclosures or attachments (if it is by email) i.e. Yours sincerely (if you have addressed the letter to a named person)

> Yours sincerely,
> Fred Knights
> Enc × 1 or Attach: CV

TIP

If you are sending an emailed cover letter, make sure attachments are detailed so the recipient can see what you should have sent with the letter.

Meeting the employer's requirements

On many job adverts and in job requirements you find employers ask for experience and this is fine for someone who has been working in a similar area of work for a year or more. But what do you do if you are just leaving school, college or university and you have little or no experience to offer? This is made worse if you are new to the job hunting game as well. What should you include to bring yourself to the employer's attention in a positive way?

Skills, experience, qualities and qualifications

When you first think of applying for a job you are often asked what relevant skills, experience and qualities you have to offer.

This can be quite difficult if you are a first-time job hunter as you may not be used to thinking about yourself in this way. You may have many good skills, qualities and experience but may not know how to put these down in a way that makes them relevant to an employer. You may have gaps in your experience or skills.

Before you can write to an employer you have to be sure what skills, experience, qualities and qualifications you may have to offer and how to get these across in a relevant way.

Skills

A skill is normally something you have learnt. For example you may be able to drive, and this is a skill you have obtained from taking a driving course. You may be able to use certain computer packages well e.g. Microsoft Word, Excel or Access, and these are skills you have acquired through going on a course or at school. Some skills may be very specific to a certain job or to a type of employment to which you are applying. This may particularly be the case after taking an apprenticeship or course at further or higher education.

There are also a range of skills known as key skills. These are skills that most employers look for and are generally helpful throughout life.

- Communication skills – this includes written, and verbal or talking skills.
- Numerical skills/working with numbers – this includes ability to complete sums.
- Information and Communication Technology – this includes any IT packages.
- Working with others – this means how you work in a team and whether you can be helpful to the team as a whole, not just good on your own.
- Improving your own learning and performance – this is looking for skills to analyse how you are doing and be able to make any adjustments required.

- Problem solving – this means being able to work things out and use your own initiative.

Sometimes key skills are assessed in school and college and levels can be given. Some employers may ask for certain key skills or qualifications showing that you have skills in a particular subject or area of work to a certain ability level. They may state that applicants must have GCSE grade C or above in Mathematics or have NVQ level 2 in Motor Vehicle Mechanics.

The importance of transferable skills. Transferable skills are simply showing that you can do something from one part of your life and that you can use it in a work setting. These are very important for the first-time job hunter. You may not have skills to offer from previous employment but may be able to show you have similar skills from other work you have done, from hobbies or voluntary experience or even from helping at an event, or within your family.

Making skills relevant. It is no good just listing your skills or interests to an employer however. Otherwise the employer will be looking at the list and thinking 'Why exactly do I need to know they are good at football?'

One common mistake made by first-time job hunters when writing about their skills is including very general skills or commonly used terms known as clichés. These immediately give the employer the impression that you may have just repeated skills directly from the advert or job specification. As a result they come across as insincere. Some examples of this are given below:

'I am interested in car maintenance and how it works. I am flexible with time and always enthusiastic. I work well in a group and on my own.'

'I am a recent graduate with excellent communication skills. I have the ability to solve problems well and can use my initiative.'

Both these examples do not show the specific skills the candidates had in relation to the job, the industry or the company for which they were applying.

Other clichés that are easily misunderstood or even attempt to convey humour in a letter should be avoided.

> 'I notice in your advert that you require a dynamic sales representative. Look no further!'

> 'Some have said that I am arrogant, but I would prefer to describe myself as an exceptional all rounder.'

The example below shows how a young person used the skills he gained from his hobby and made it relevant to the job he was applying for.

Dear Mr Smith

Re: Junior Web/Graphic Design apprenticeship vacancy

I am writing with reference to the junior web/graphic designer vacancy you have advertised on your website.

I am a person interested in graphic and web design and have gained the following skills over a period of years.

Lists relevant skills to the advert

- Computer literacy in Microsoft Office and other processing programs.
- Adobe Photoshop CS3 experience which includes digital design work, photo manipulation and illustration.
- Front page/Web expression 2. I have worked on developing my own online portfolio website using specialist software. This can be viewed on my website www.jkrealdesigns.co.uk.
- My website also shows skills in graphic design, photography, illustration, web design and 3D Sculpture work.

Refers to website so employer can see more skills

I understand your company has a wide client base and deals with a wide range of design aspects such as web design, graphics, and digital print. This would be particularly interesting to me as it would allow me to learn new skills while also working. I am highly motivated and IT is my real passion in life. I am largely self-taught and would offer your company the chance to train me to your requirements.

Good research, relates skills to employer's business

I attach my Curriculum Vitae for your consideration. Please visit my website to see examples of my work. I would be happy to come for an interview or informal meeting at a time that suits you.

Yours sincerely,

James Keen

Enc × 1

In this example James had gained most of his experience through his hobby and general interest and not at school or through work experience. As such much of his skills were self-taught. However, he was able to show the employer what skills he had and could demonstrate these appropriately by referring the employer to his website. He made his hobby relevant to the position and could demonstrate he had relevant skills asked for in the advert.

You need to show how you came by these skills and how they can be used in the job. James has made his skills relevant by showing that he knows what the employer actually does, and therefore how he may be useful to them.

James chose in his cover letter to bullet point his skills. This isn't necessary in many cases but as the requirement of this job involved lots of specific skills, this was one way of presenting the information in an easy to read style. However, this approach would not look good in a handwritten letter.

Experience

You can gain experience through previous jobs you have had and been paid to do. This is known as employment experience.

Another way of getting experience to help you with job applications is to undertake some work experience. Work experience and voluntary experience are not paid, although expenses may be offered. Work experience is done in Years 10 and 11 at school for a couple of weeks. For this you may be asked to find your own placement. However, whether you are applying for a work experience placement while still at school or voluntary experience to gain experience there is a similar process to follow.

First you will need to find out which employers may offer you the experience you are looking for and find out their details. This can be initially daunting and often as with work experience you may be inclined to take the easiest option, asking someone you know. This may be helpful if they are in a type of employment you want to go into but if not, it will be of little help.

It is better if you can look for opportunities that will help you develop important knowledge and experience about an area in which you really want to work. Look at the example given on p. 51 where Nathan is looking for work experience with a local employer.

EXAMPLE

Nathan is looking to have a career in sport. He doesn't know exactly what yet. He has played football and cricket for some county sides but suffered an injury last year that has proved to be a problem. After seeing his personal adviser at school he realised that there were many other jobs in sport such as teaching and being a sports development officer which he could still do.

He doesn't know anything about sports development so he has decided this would be something he would be interested in.

Nathan's first challenge is to find an employer who will be willing to take him for his work experience. Initially he doesn't know where to start but he asks around and then a teacher suggests to him that it might be worth contacting the local council to see if they run activities for children in the area.

He goes to his library as he is unsure what councils do and asks if there is a department that covers sports in the community. The lady on the information desks tells him that there is a particular department of the district council that covers sports development. He obtains a phone number and contact details for Mrs V. Nice who heads up that department.

He phones Mrs Nice the next day and she isn't in so he leaves a message asking her to phone him when she can on his mobile number. The next day comes and he doesn't hear from her. So he rings again and leaves another message. The next day Mrs Nice phones him back.

The conversation is transcribed overleaf.

Mrs Nice:	Hello is that Nathan, you phoned me yesterday and I was out of the office all day. How can I help you?
Nathan:	I am looking for somewhere to do my work experience. I am in Year 11 at Hawthorn Comprehensive and I need to get two weeks' work experience in May. I would really like to know more about sports development as I am interested in sport and think I might want to go into this as a career.
Mrs Nice:	What weeks would you be looking at coming?
Nathan:	It would be the 11th to the 22nd of May 2009.
Mrs Nice:	That seems to be fine – there will be quite a lot of planning taking place then because of National Sports Week at the end of June, but if you don't mind it being busy then I'm sure we can fit you in. If you could write a letter to me so I have your request in writing then I will see about arranging a member of the team to look after you.
Nathan:	That would be great. Also would it possible to have the placement confirmed in writing from you as I need to show the careers co-ordinator that I've got the placement sorted.
Mrs Nice:	No problem, I look forward to hearing from you soon. Bye.

Nathan has successfully managed to secure a placement. He didn't give up when Mrs Nice didn't phone back the first time. This is very important as you may have to make several phone calls before you get through to the right person or they to get back to you. But don't pester!

Nathan explains what he is looking for in a polite way. He shows his enthusiasm and gives a good reason why he wants to come to the employer. He is able to express to the employer that he also needs the placement confirmed in writing for the school.

Now Nathan needs to write his cover letter as requested by Mrs V. Nice. This is how he does it.

36 Ambition Street
Salisbury
Wiltshire
SP4 3DA

15 November 2008

Mrs V Nice
Principal Sports Development Officer
Community Initiatives
Salisbury District Council
Salisbury
SP2 1BU

Makes clear why he is writing
and the school he is at

Good reference

Dear Mrs Nice

Re: Work experience 11–22 May 2009

I am writing to you as a pupil in Year 11 of Hawthorn Comprehensive School in Salisbury. I am looking to gain two weeks' work experience from 11 May to 22 May 2009. As part of this I am encouraged to find an employer whose work I am interested in and who would be prepared to have me and show me aspects of what they do.

I am very keen on sport and have played at county level in both football and cricket. I work well in teams and this is shown by the fact I have represented the school football team for the last 5 years. I enjoy coaching my younger brother in football and think that working in sport with children might be something I would enjoy. I am doing well at GCSEs and my favourite subjects include PE and Biology.

Shows his relevant
interests at school

I think coming to the district council would help me get a clearer idea of what is involved in sports development as a career and how sport can play a role in the community. I am physically fit other than a past ankle injury, keen to learn and enthusiastic about sport. If I were to gain the work experience with your department then this would help me when I come to look at future career goals and when I fill in my college application form.

I have a deadline of 31 January for my choice of employer to be confirmed. This needs to be in writing to me.

Relates his work experience
placement to long term career idea

With thanks for your consideration.

Yours sincerely,

Nathan Right

Asks what he needs the
employer to do and when

- This example shows how Nathan has produced a well researched and carefully constructed letter as Mrs Nice has asked him to do. It shows both the research he has undertaken and also the clear structure to each of the paragraphs.
- Nathan has investigated beforehand that the employer may be willing to give him a go and therefore has the necessary details to do a targeted letter. This is far more likely to be successful than if Nathan had just sent a general or speculative letter to the department.
- Nathan's letter is clear and he shows in the first paragraph why he is writing. He gives the details to the employer of how long the placement would be and what experience he is looking for.
- In the second paragraph he states what relevant skills he has, for example he is a county player, and what experience he has, that particularly relates to helping children with sport. He also states how he is doing at GCSE and that he enjoys subjects relating to sport i.e. PE and Biology. This gives the employer the impression he is interested in sport and has some sound and relevant subjects and skills to back up his application.
- In the third paragraph he says why he wants to come particularly to this employer and what knowledge he hopes to gain from the placement. He also states some qualities about himself; that he is keen to learn and, most importantly, that he is enthusiastic about sport. The employer will be looking for these qualities and this will make the placement easier for them. Nathan shows the employer how this placement will help him in future college applications and the employer can see that not only is Nathan serious about his work placement but that he has also thought through how he will use his experience.

Personal qualities

Personal qualities can often be described as something special or good about you as a person that you have to offer. An employer may be looking for certain types of personal qualities that will mean you will fit into the work environment well. Below are some of the sorts of personal qualities that an employer might expect to see.

enthusiastic	dedicated	able to work well in a team
passionate	motivated	use initiative
willing/keen to learn	honest	keep calm under pressure
flexible/can adapt to change	reliable	determination to succeed

You must look to put personal qualities in context so that you don't merely list them. The best way of doing this is to give an example. James does this in his letter by saying that IT is his passion in life and giving examples of his work (p. 49). Nathan does this in his letter by showing he works well in teams as he has represented his school football team for the last 5 years.

TIP

Don't sound too good to be true.

It is important when expressing your personal qualities that they come across in the letter as genuine. There is no point in listing a number of qualities just because you think they sound good. They have to come from you and match what the employer is looking for. As one recruiter told me:

> 'I once had a letter from someone who expressed that they were dynamic, enthusiastic, the best that banking had to offer. My first question to myself was then why haven't they got a job? I was a bit suspicious – it just didn't sound right.'

Qualifications

You will know the qualifications you have. If you haven't yet got the result from an exam you can't include this in your qualifications unless you can back up an expected result by proof. This would be through marks in your course-work so far or your predicted degree grade as given by a tutor.

It is best to highlight qualifications you have that fit in with the employer's requirements. If you have obvious gaps in qualifications then it is important to think about how you can sell what you do have positively and state you are willing to undergo further training. Notice how Nathan did this in his letter to the employer. If you are unsure how to go about getting certain skills or qualifications then it is always worth seeking advice from one of the agencies offering advice and guidance listed in the resource section.

You'll need to think carefully what qualifications to include as you only have room for one or two. A local recruiter pointed out some of the less useful types of qualifications they have seen in cover letters and CVs.

'In the past, everyone put down their swimming certificates they got a school. What we want to see is qualifications that are relevant to the job. A swimming certificate is fine if you are going to be a life guard but not much use for insurance frankly.'

Your personal planner

The secret of a winning cover letter is to be able to pick out two or three skills and qualities (maximum) to put in your letter which are most relevant to this employer and opportunity. You don't want to list loads as these may well be included in your CV or application form. Again, the experience and qualifications you include should be an example of each skill/quality that you've chosen to highlight in your letter.

Skills	2 of my top skills I can offer with examples	How this relates to the employer
Experience/interest	An example of experience or interests I have	How this relates to the employer
Personal qualities	2 examples of personal qualities I have	How these relate to the employer
Qualifications	2 qualifications I have	How these relate to employer/job

Use the planner above to help you write down your skills, experience, qualities and qualifications for your cover letter.

The secret to getting the information right in any cover letter is tailoring it the person you are writing to, showing them you are genuinely interested in them and their business. You now have the seven parts of the cover letter to guide you as to what information to put where. The five key elements (listed on pp. 31–9) help underpin any information you include to make sure your letter leaves just the right impression.

5

Different cover letters for different jobs

During this chapter we will look at the different types of jobs that you might be applying to and how to tailor your cover letter accordingly.

This will include advice on how to create:

- cover letters to apply for an apprenticeship
- letters for first time graduates applying to a national graduate trainee position
- letters for industries that may be a bit more individual, like those in the creative industries such as art and design and music.

A national apprenticeship qualification

An apprenticeship is a way of working and learning at the same time and being paid a wage for doing so. The apprentice goes to work for an employer and then goes to a learning provider to do training for nationally recognised qualifications. There are 180 apprenticeships available covering 80 sectors of industry and commerce. One way of finding out if there is an apprenticeship offered in the career area you are interested in is to go to the website www.apprenticeships.org.uk.

Many Connexions centres will have apprenticeships adverts on the vacancy part of their websites, and personal advisers in schools and colleges will also be able to tell you what is available. It is worth going to your local Connexions website to see what is available. See the resources section for more details on this and the apprenticeship hotline.

Apprenticeships are a good way of gaining relevant qualifications and experience while working and often include learning about key skills. Apprenticeships help you gain National Vocational Qualifications (NVQs) or technical certificates.

If you are under 16 years old, Young Apprenticeships offer young people aged 14–16 opportunity to go on a work based learning programme. This involves work experience for 50 days within a certain industry sector. This can really help you get ahead before you come to do it for real after you are 16 years old. If you are interested in this it is worth speaking to a connexions adviser about what availability there is in your local area.

How does the application process work?

Applying through AVMS

Most apprenticeships applications can now go through AVMS. This is a centralised vacancy matching service which is accessed through the website www.apprenticeships.org.uk. For this only one application from is filled in online after you register. The form is then used to automatically alert you to vacancies in the areas of work you are looking for. The registration is free and you are given a couple of choice of areas of work you are interested in.

In this case a cover letter isn't used for the initial application although certain vacancies may require a covering letter in a later stage of an individual vacancy application depending on what the employer/provider has specified. You can also search for learning providers in your area through the site, subscribe to the newsletter and look at apprenticeship case-studies.

This way of applying for apprenticeships is fairly quick and useful but it may be that you are not sure which areas of work you wish to apply for, or that you need help with applying, or you don't want to use or are not able to use an online system.

Other ways to apply for apprenticeships

It may be that you see a vacancy for an apprenticeship on a local Connexions website. You may hear of one through talking to an adviser at a connexions centre. You may see a vacancy advertised directly from the company itself through the local jobs section of a local paper or from an online job search site. Once you have made the initial contact with an employer or the connexions centre that is shown on the vacancy, they will send you information about the vacancy and direct you how to apply.

 It is worth looking at the company website before you ring for any further details as some have answers to the most popular questions online. Any information you gain from the website can help you in your cover letter.

Some apprenticeships are advertised by the employer direct and they will ask you to fill in an online application or send a CV and cover letter to a particular person. Other vacancies will be handled by Connexions or may direct you first to apply to a learning provider who is handling the vacancy on behalf of the employer. Learning providers offer training to employers and often handle vacancies on their behalf. The providers are often focused on industry areas in which they specialise.

This may mean that you won't know who the company is that you are applying to, but only the learning provider's details. Selection may involve both interviews and assessment with a provider and the employer.

Let us look at an example of an advert for an administrative assistant apprenticeship. Rebecca White has recently left school in Year 11. She has seen this advert on her local Connexions website under vacancies. She decides she is going to apply.

ADMINISTRATIVE ASSISTANT

CONNEXIONS SOUTH
All Opportunities Open to Males and Females

Ref no: 1247

Location: Northgate Street, Little Church, Surrey

Wages: Apprentice rate – £80 pwk minimum to start

Job description
APPRENTICESHIP – general administration/
office duties to include data inputting, photocopying, filing, faxing,
answering telephone, post.

Qualifications and qualities
A good level/understanding of literacy and numeracy required.
Good IT/computer skills required – knowledge of Excel useful
but training provided.

Hours
37 hours per week. Monday–Friday, 5 day week.

Training
In-house training plus training leading to
NVQ 2 Administration award via OTS.

Other Information
Able to work as part of a team.

To apply
Send a cover letter and CV to Jane Hopkins, OTS, Training Street,
Big Church, Surrey, GU7 4XT or email a cover letter and
CV to otsplacements@yahoo.co.uk.

Contact: Mrs Jane Hopkins, Recruitment Co-ordinator, OTS
Tel: 222234   **Fax:** 222235
Company name: To be disclosed at the OTS interview

Rebecca's cover letter

Full address given

7 Lyme Road
Cherry Tree Avenue
Surrey
GU14 7DT
Email: R.White@emailgoogle.com

3 July 2009

Mrs Jane Hopkins
Learning Co-ordinator
Office Training Services
Training Street
Big Church
Surrey
GU7 4XT

She addresses the letter to the work based learning provider

She states which vacancy

Dear Mrs Hopkins

shows career goals

Re: Administrative Assistant Apprenticeship – vacancy no: 1247

I was particularly interested to see a vacancy advertised on the Connexions South website this week for an administrative assistant. I have recently left school after completing my GCSEs. I would like to become a secretary and see this opportunity as a first step towards this goal.

One of the GCSEs I most enjoyed at school was Business Administration. Throughout the course I showed an ability to organise and present my work effectively. I am competent in Microsoft Word, Excel and use of the internet. I have represented the school at a recent enterprise event which required me to work as part of a team to deliver a presentation.

Excellent demonstration of personal qualities for employer

I would like to train with Office Training Services to gain my National Vocational Qualification level 2 in Business Administration. I would like an apprenticeship as I am keen to gain as much practical experience as possible. I live locally with easy access to bus routes to the north side of town.

The learning provider will want to know if she can get to the employer

I attach my Curriculum Vitae for your consideration. I am contactable at the above address any time except for 17–23 August when I am away on holiday in Cornwall. I look forward to hearing from you shortly.

Yours sincerely,

Rebecca White

Enclosed × 1

- Rebecca addresses the letter correctly to the training provider. She has clearly read the instructions on the advert. She also puts a clear reference on the letter. This is very important as the learning provider has lots of different vacancies they are handling on behalf of employers.
- Rebecca starts strongly saying she is particularly interested in the vacancy and how this vacancy is part of her long term goal to become a secretary.
- Rebecca has shown in this cover letter to the learning provider that she is keen to do an apprenticeship. She shows that she understands what an apprenticeship is in the letter and why she feels this is something she wants to do.
- Rebecca does not include details of the employer as this vacancy is being handled by the learning provider. She does however point out in the letter that she has taken business administration at school and what skills, qualities she has to offer the learning provider. The learning provider will be looking for these to match those requested by the employer.
- The learning provider wants to know that Rebecca has the interest and that she is able to take on the training they will be offering. Rebecca states she understands the training on offer and would be interested in doing the NVQ level 2.
- Rebecca shows the training provider she can get to the employer who is on the other side of town. This is important as the training provider needs to make sure she can get to them and the employer.
- Lastly, Rebecca points the learning provider towards her CV. Her Curriculum Vitae is tailored to bring out her qualifications, experience, qualities and skills mentioned in this vacancy.

Rebecca has made the choice to send her letter by post rather than email it with her CV. She has chosen to do this as she feels this will show her employer better that she can put together a good business letter and CV and send these out in the post. She wanted to show just how nicely she could present the letter.

A postal application is one of the options given on the advert so this is appropriate. However, if Rebecca had sent it via email it would have been important in this vacancy for a full letter to have been attached along with her CV so that it comes across just like a letter sent in the post in the same business-like fashion.

TIP

Make sure you read carefully what the learning provider or employer want. If you are asked for a cover letter then it must be a proper letter not a quick email.

If the advert had been directed to the employer and had included the employer's details, her cover letter may have looked like this.

---

7 Lyme Road
Cherry Tree Avenue
Surrey
GV14 7DT
Email: R.White@emailgoogle.com

3 July 2009

Mr J Boss
Managing Director   *Rebecca addresses the letter directly to the employer*
Best Insurance
Insurance House
Northgate Street
Little Church
Surrey
GV5 4ST

Tells employer where she saw the advert

Dear Mr Boss

Re: Administrative Assistant Apprenticeship – vacancy no: 1247

I was particularly interested to see a vacancy advertised on the Connexions South website this week for an administrative assistant. I have recently left school after completing my GCSEs. I would like to become a secretary and see this opportunity as a first step towards this goal.

One of the GCSEs I most enjoyed at school was Business Administration. Throughout the course I showed a natural ability to organise and present my work effectively. I am competent in Microsoft Word, Excel and use of the internet. I have represented the school at a recent enterprise event which required me to work as part of a team to deliver a presentation.

I notice from your advert the apprenticeship would include training. I would very much like to train for a National Vocational Qualification Level 2 in Business Administration. I would like an apprenticeship as I am keen to gain as much practical experience as possible.

I would really like to work for Best Insurance as it has a very good reputation both locally and nationally. I know that it recently won the Insurance of the Year award. I am aware that your apprenticeship training scheme is considered very comprehensive and would give me lots of experience across different areas of administration.

This shows Rebecca has been on the employer's website and researched the company

I attach my Curriculum Vitae for your consideration. I am contactable at the above address any time except for 17–23 August when I am away on holiday in Cornwall. I look forward to hearing from you shortly.

Yours sincerely,

Rebecca White

Enclosed × 1

Rebecca here addresses the letter directly to the company and the name given on the vacancy.

Rebecca has put in a paragraph here about the company itself, Best Insurance. She researched the company website and found that their training scheme is considered one of the best nationally because it allows lots of areas of administration to be covered. She puts this into her letter to show that she has real knowledge about the company and has bothered to do some research.

The company are impressed with Rebecca's efforts, her enthusiasm and her attention to detail. They offer her an interview and then one of the three apprenticeship positions in the company.

A cover letter for a graduate trainee position

Graduate trainee positions are often advertised in university careers centres, or through websites that are designed specifically for helping graduates to apply for jobs, such as the Prospects website www.prospects.ac.uk. A specific university may have notices on their own website telling graduates of possible careers events and the 'milkround' where companies come to the university to find possible graduate trainees. Some of the graduate websites such as Prospects will also advertise part-time, full-time and temporary job vacancies which can prove useful if you are trying to get experience. For more information on this go to the resources section at the back of this book.

Lots of universities may also have a job shop which is a place on campus where undergraduates can find jobs. Most students now have to work and study at the same time to make things easier financially. This kind of temporary work should not be underplayed as it gives graduates vital key skills that make them more employable at the end of their study.

Graduate traineeships – what are they?

Some graduate jobs are specifically tailored to a course of study or profession. Subjects such as medicine or law will be focused on jobs in specific fields. These types of careers will often have set requirements and designated application routes.

Other degrees however may be used to apply for a variety of jobs that are not subject specific. These are general graduate vacancies and graduate traineeships where the subject studied is not as important as the qualities and abilities of the graduate. These general graduate vacancies allow companies to 'fast track' or train graduates up into positions of responsibility.

It is very important when you are applying for a graduate traineeship that you bother to research both the training scheme and the company. You should also be aware of all aspects of a company, e.g. is it international/global, and whether the company you are applying to is one part of a group offering different products and services. This kind of awareness is vital to success.

Let's look at the example below for a graduate traineeship opportunity.

Susan Ready has been an undergraduate for two years. She is now in her final year and is thinking of applying for graduate vacancies. She has been to the careers centre to find out about what graduate vacancies she might apply for. She has been studying a business management degree which will lead to a Bachelor of Science. She is hopeful of getting a good grade in this degree, probably an upper second class.

She would like to go on a fast track graduate scheme and would really like to travel in her work. She knows that graduate traineeships will be competitive as graduates from throughout the country can apply, but she is confident she has something special to offer.

The careers adviser tells her that there is a new graduate traineeship running this year by an international insurance company called Bright Insurance. Bright Insurance are already very well known throughout the world as a massive insurance group but they are advertising this year for their Bright Sparks United Arab Emirates Scheme which is based in Dubai. The careers adviser knows that the scheme is looking for good quality graduates with an interest in business. She suggests Susan take a look at their website and the details about the scheme on their careers vacancy board.

After looking at the website Susan realises that the company is looking for graduates with an interest in insurance and finance. She has taken an option which gives her a certificate approved by the Chartered Insurance Institute and feels this might give her an edge over other candidates. She also really likes the idea of working in Dubai. Susan notes that the first stage of the application is to email a cover letter with a completed application form back to the main UK base of the company in Guildford.

She sends off the following cover letter via email as requested.

Susan's cover letter

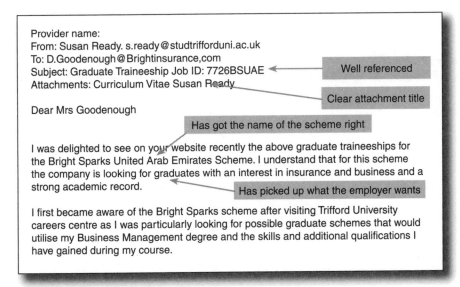

Points out relevant qualifications and knowledge

In particular I believe that the Certificate of Insurance recognised by the Chartered Insurance Institute that I have gained as part of the degree may be of interest to you. I have a strong overall academic record and am expecting an upper second class degree. I also received the highest marks in the second year for my Marketing project on global branding. I have, as a result of research for this project, a desire to work for a global company and to work in the heart of financial centres around the world.

This helps her stand out

I am aware of Bright Insurance as a global leader in the insurance industry that offers a wide range of financial products including loans and mortgages as well as both commercial and private insurance. It offers 'insurance for the man and mankind'. In terms of these core values of business undertaken by Bright Insurance I feel that my degree course has given me a solid foundation, including customer service, through virtual and online mediums, business accounting and economics, and global strategic management.

She knows what type of company it is and what it does

Has done her research

I am attracted to the Bright Sparks training scheme because the 18 month programme includes experiencing all aspects of the business from the bottom up and this allows me to really gain practical experience. Past employment during the summer vacation last year at Bush Finance helped me gain this kind of hands on experience and increase my skills. These included customer service over the phone including taking international calls, building relationships with clients, and keeping accurate database records.

Relates skills to the job

I hope that my Curriculum Vitae attached illustrates to you my potential to perform well on the training scheme and make a real difference to the firm. I am available for interview any time except during the last two weeks of June when I am undertaking my final exams.

Yours sincerely,

Susan Ready

- In the email, Susan has written a proper letter to bring out all the aspects about of her relevant skills, experience, qualities and qualifications that she has to offer.
- She has stated where she saw the advert and which university she is attending. She starts strongly with enthusiasm and by recognising what the Bright Sparks scheme is about.

- She makes sure that her CII qualifications are mentioned, as these are directly relevant to the company, and picks up on requirements of a good academic background quoted in the advert.
- In the third paragraph Susan uses the chance to show she has read the motto of the company and knows its core values and business areas. She shows how her degree course ties in with these areas of business.
- She demonstrates in the fourth paragraph that she is aware of what the scheme offers and how long it is for. She points out to the employer that she has had previous relevant experience over the summer in a financial company and has gained relevant transferable skills. She worked in a call centre and importantly has shown what this has taught her.
- Lastly she says when she is available and indicates to the employer to look at he CV.

A cover letter for a part-time job application

Mike is presently at college doing a music technology course. He is enjoying his course but is looking now to get some relevant employment experience and also earn some money to keep his motorbike on the road.

He sees the advert overleaf in a local music shop window and thinks this might be the opportunity for him.

CLASHES MUSIC STORE

STORE ASSISTANT

Job description

General assistant required to work at
weekends in local city centre store.

Job Duties

Serving and advising customers on music selection,
display and ordering of stock.

Hours

Saturdays and Sundays 8.30-5.30; 16 hours per week
with 2×45 min lunch break and two breaks

Qualities required

Must have some interest in music.
Retail experience preferred but training will be given.
Polite and customer friendly.

To apply

Please send a cover letter and CV to Sam James, Clashes Music
Store, St Crispin's Street, Northampton NX1 2ET

Mike is attracted to the advert as he is into music and also feels that the job may help his career by keeping him familiar with the local alternative music scene and local contacts.

He goes into the shop to ask the manager about the job. He finds out that the manager has similar interests in music to him and that he has just been to a recent music festival which Mike also attended.

He goes away much more encouraged and writes the following cover letter.

Mike's cover letter

Address is formal and correct

2 Bracken Close Woodlands
Hackleton
Northampton
NX9 1UR

6 June 2009

Mr Sam Jones
Clashes Music Store
St Crispin's Street
Northampton
NX1 2ET

Although he has met Sam he still addresses the letter formally and correctly

Mike has met Sam and has been told he can address the letter using his first name

Dear Sam

Re: Store Assistant Position

He uses the employer's job title

Thank you for seeing me yesterday about the position for store assistant. As I said I am interested in this position as I have a long standing interest in music and feel that this position would also fit in well with my current study.

Great hook – Mike reminds Sam who he is

I am currently studying a BTEC Music Technology Diploma at Northampton College. In addition to this I also play the drums to grade 7 standard, and the harmonica. I am committed to the local music scene, attending festivals and any concerts I can get to. I am a subscriber to *Independent Music Magazine*.

This is a great way to show his interest

I have done some casual work for my uncle before on his fruit and vegetable stall in the city centre which included talking to customers, taking money and helping with display of the produce. I am hardworking and willing to learn.

Shows relevant skills

I think that working for Clashes would be a job I would love which would offer me valuable experience. I know the store is widely regarded in the city and surrounding area as one of the best independent stockists of music. It offers a very personal and quality experience for customers which I would like to be a part of.

He shows he really knows what Clashes is about

I enclosed my CV for your attention. I am available to start from the beginning of July.

I look forward to hearing from you.

He shows when he is available

Best Wishes,

Mike can get away with this ending as he knows Sam

Mike Chan
Enc × 1

- The manager is pleased with the letter he receives from Mike and his quick response. This helps him remember Mike and their conversation about the festival.
- He also gets the impression that Mike is genuinely interested in music. He gets this from the fact that Mike plays instruments and reads a well known magazine. This impresses him and he feels that Mike may have knowledge that can be used when serving customers.
- Mike has shown he has relevant skills serving the public although not in music retail. Sam likes his enthusiastic attitude.
- The most striking thing Sam notices is that this would be a job that Mike wants. He has shown he 'gets' what Clashes is all about. It isn't a typical retail music store but very much appeals to a dedicated market of committed fans. Mike has shown he understands this and Sam feels that he is just the sort of person he is looking for.

 TIP Use of first names and more relaxed endings are fine if you have been asked to address the letter as such or if you know the person well. If however, you are in any doubt stick to formal endings.

This advert was in a shop window. This doesn't mean however that a laid-back approach to applying will do. Any application to this advert has to be of a high standard just as if the ad was placed in a paper or on a website.

Any employer advertising part-time work will expect to be answered in a professional manner, just as you would for a full-time position.

Cover letters for full-time job applications

Sian has recently moved to Devon and is looking for her first full-time job. She hasn't had much luck and doesn't feel she knows Devon very well. She hasn't really got much employment experience and left school after GCSEs. She is not very confident, quite shy and suffers from severe asthma. Sian loves children, and while in Cardiff worked a few hours a week as a helper at a local play group.

She goes into a learning centre in Devon and there an adviser shows her some of the learning options open to her as well as ideas to help her job search. Sian finds an advert in the local paper she finds in the library.

ROCKING HORSE NURSERY CENTRE
NURSERY ASSISTANT NA0182/272

£9,000–£12,500

37 hours per week, term time plus 1 week

We are looking to appoint a motivated and understanding key staff member to our nursery centre for September 2009.

Recent experience of young children aged between 6 months and 4 years is essential. Qualifications in the care of young children are not essential but a willingness to undertake further training as required would be expected.

We are seeking most of all a caring and understanding individual. Candidates should be calm and able to encourage young children as well as taking an interest in the needs of all children and adapt to any special needs.

This post is subject to appropriate CRB clearance.

To apply: Send a letter of interest to Mrs Fiona Keeble, Rocking Horse Nursery Centre, Cliff Avenue, Bigbury, Devon, TQ3 4XZ

The job advert appeals to Sian as it doesn't say that she has to have specific qualifications in childcare or previous experience working as a teaching assistant. She decided to ring up Mrs Keeble and find out more about the position. Mrs Keeble offers the chance for Sian to come and see the nursery centre that afternoon. Sian is quite nervous but her sister persuades her to go down and look at it. She gets on well with Mrs Keeble and finds out that the centre has quite a few children with asthma like her and other special needs which really interests her. Mrs Keeble asks her to write her a letter to express her interest.

Sian's cover letter

The Old Farm
Birch Tree Lane
Bigbury
Devon
TQ3 1TR

13 June 2009

Mrs F Keeble
Rocking Horse Nursery Centre
Cliff Avenue
Bigbury
Devon
TQ3 4XZ

> Addresses the letter as the advert requests

Dear Mrs Keeble

> Uses the correct reference

Re: Nursery Assistant NA0182/272

> Reminds the manager of her visit – great hook

I was delighted to see your advert for a nursery assistant at your centre. Thank you for showing me around on Wednesday. I really liked the centre as it was so friendly. I thought the new outdoor mini play area was brilliant.

> Enthusiastic start

I have recently moved to Devon and am looking for my first full-time job in early years care. I have worked before at a playgroup in Cardiff for 11 months which I loved. The play group was for children from the ages of 1–3 years of age. I would really like to go on to train to be a nursery assistant while also working. I feel working for the Rocking Horse Nursery Centre would give me this chance.

> Sian says how this job will help her career aims

While at the playgroup I worked with a number of children who had particular needs. This included one little boy who had ADHD and a little girl with severe eczema. I learnt that by helping the children to be included in activities, giving them praise and remaining calm if they were upset really helped the children to enjoy the playgroup.

I myself suffer from asthma and I have found that often it is the tiniest thing or acting in time that proves to help the most. For example with the little boy I taught him a game involving counting stars which he loved and helped him settle. With the little girl I found that keeping her away from the windows made her less itchy.

> Sian decided to mention her own disability but makes it a positive point

I notice that the nursery won an award last year for best practice. I think this is a wonderful achievement. I would very much like to be a part of this kind of team that makes every child feel special.

I look forward to hearing from you.

> Shows knowledge of the centre and great use of this for a strong ending

Yours sincerely,

Sian Williams

- Sian's letter has something that none of the other letters that Mrs Keeble receives have. Sian shows through her examples that she really has the ability to work out how to adapt her approach to different children's needs. This strikes Mrs Keeble immediately.
- Sian hasn't got lots of qualifications or massive experience. But her letter shows her to be a caring and very astute candidate.
- Sian has made the difficult decision to highlight in the letter her disability but she has done so in a very positive way. Showing what she has learnt from it and overcome through it.
- Sian is also clear about wanting to work with children and has a particular career goal in mind which this job is entirely suitable for.

What this example shows is that no matter what your previous experience, qualifications or disability, by making extra effort and thinking carefully about the most important aspects of a job can make your tailored letter the winning one.

Cover letters with a difference – the WOW factor

There are some situations and for some industries where deviating from the normal standard cover letter template and traditional style CV can be acceptable or even beneficial. Often these are for jobs in the creative industries such as art and design, performing arts or music.

It is very important if you do intend to do this that you are sure that this will be acceptable. The key to this is knowing who you are sending it to. For example if you are sending a cover letter and CV to a creative director in a company then something unexpected or different might be fine as long as they can appreciate what you are doing. If you are sending it to the human resources manager you can bet that being overly creative might not work, and could actually work against you.

It can be really beneficial to talk to employers in the industry first to make sure your application is targeted correctly and will stand out in a good way. Often applications for positions in graphic design, animation and film, games design, music and performing arts can be highly competitive and this extra research can make the difference.

Art students should know that creative directors like to see portfolios or a few examples of their work to get a feel of their style and whether it will fit their organisation. As art is so personal it may not be a decision that an artist or designer has talent or not. Rather, that it is not the type of talent they are looking for.

Therefore in the creative industries preparation on constructing a high standard of e-portfolio and/or creative CV and targeting this correctly to employers is crucial. It has to be faultless in its presentation (as presentation is a main factor in the art and design world), well targeted and have that wow factor in the first 7 seconds of a director looking at it instead of 'oh how disappointing'.

Likewise a film or animation company may be looking for a show reel or animation clip to show the kinds of work you have undertaken. You may be applying to quite small companies and for initially short-term or temporary contracts to gain further experience.

Often in jobs in the creative arts, past performance and client base is key to future success. Therefore any chance of getting any type of real experience, whether temporary, paid, voluntary, part-time or as an internship, should be grabbed as this will put your application ahead of the rest. You can sell yourself through recommendation and this is a winning formula for the creative sector.

Let's look at the letter below to get an idea of tailoring a cover letter for a fashion design student.

Provider name
From: Sophie Glaser
To: Katherine@emaildesignsforlife.co.uk
Subject: Graduate Outerwear Designer vacancy ← — — — Clear subject heading
Attachments: CV and 3 JPEGs of work.

Careful attention to
advert requirements

Dear Miss Dye

I was pleased to see your recent advert on the Prospects website for a graduate outerwear designer. I notice from the advert that you require recent outerwear experience.

During my last year at university I have been involved with a local company, Springboard Designers, who offered me a work placement. This involved specifically designing a trench style coat for their winter collection. As part of this I had experience of the whole design process from original sketch, through regular and technical sketches to sample garments.

Targets experience to job

During my course I have gained competency in programs such as Adobe Photoshop and Illustrator. I took part in the local GDT Fashion exhibition held at the Assembly Hall and gained recognition by winning the best design newcomer award. I have also taken part in exhibitions inside the university and been an ambassador for my course where I have represented the university to the wider business community.

Relevant skills

I feel that I could offer Designs for Life vibrant and wearable women's outer clothing that combines practicality with affordability. I feel that the company is right at the cutting edge of new fashion and bringing catwalk designs to the middle income market.

I attach my CV with JPEGs of a couple of designs as requested. I look forward to hearing from you soon.

Yours sincerely,

Sophie Glaser   Attached in right format.
Attach: × 4

Sophie, in this letter, has targeted her experience to that required by the employer and emphasised her achievements on the course. This shows the employer that she has read the advert well and taken note of what is required. She has followed instructions and given the employer attachments in JPEG format of her designs. Her basic cover letter emphasises experience, as this is what the employer wants, and she lets her designs show her skills.

6

How the cover letter works with your CV

A cover letter is a way of introducing yourself hopefully in a good way to an employer. In a cover letter you want the employer to look at the letter and think yes; I want to know more. If your cover letter has your CV attached or enclosed you want the employer to be impressed enough to go on and read your CV.

It is really important that both your cover letter and your CV are of a high standard. They need to both be well targeted, nicely presented and work well together. If your cover letter isn't good enough the employer won't get to the CV. If the CV isn't good enough then the employer won't be putting your application on the Yes pile for interview.

In this chapter I give examples of both cover letters and CVs. The reason for this is that any cover letter sent should complement the CV that goes with it. They work together and this is reflected in the examples used.

By the end of this chapter you will be clear on:

- what information a cover letter gives that a CV does not
- what to beware of when sending a cover letter with your CV
- what makes a good and bad CV and cover letter combination.

If you want to know more about writing a CV then see another book in the series called *Winning CVs for First-time Job Hunters,* also published by Trotman.

What is a CV?

A CV or, in the full Latin, Curriculum Vitae means literally 'course of life'; or in other words the story of your life detailing the main parts including education, employment or work experience, specific skills and qualifications and interests. Sometimes it may be called a resume.

A CV is a very useful tool. It is used for two main types of application. Firstly, in speculative applications where you are sending a CV on the off-chance that there is or may shortly be opportunities for you at an employer or similar types of employers. Secondly, in specifically targeted CVs which are responding to a particular advert or vacancy.

CVs are a quick and easy way for an employer to work out whether you have the right education, employment history, set of skills and the qualities they are looking for. As it is quick to read, it should never be more than 2 sides of A4.

The dangers of sending a CV and a cover letter together

CVs can really clinch a job interview for you. However, CVs sent with cover letters have a number of inbuilt dangers to them.

* The cover letter with a CV merely repeats information in the CV.
* The cover letter is targeted and the CV isn't. This is a particular danger with speculative letters where a CV is attached but hasn't been updated or made relevant.
* The cover letter and CV are seen as two different items. They do not work together, and do not help each other to sell the candidate for a position.
* The cover letter is made up as a quick after thought and has errors in it and looks careless.

The aim of a cover letter that is sent with a CV

The aim of a cover letter with a CV is to:

* set the scene or show the employer why you are sending them your CV

- get the employer or recruiter to read the CV
- complement the CV in style, language, accuracy. They must look like they belong together and sing the same tune.
- point out the most important aspects of yourself which you wish the employer to be drawn to. This doesn't mean repeating what is in your person statement on the CV. It means giving a few snippets of highly targeted relevant information which are then backed up by information in your CV.

Getting a CV and cover letter to work together is quite an art and takes time and practise. However, it is worth the extra effort. It is a bit like going to see your favourite band in concert and then getting there to find the main vocalist was singing a different set of songs to what the band was playing. You come out with the overall impression – what was that about?

A bad CV and cover letter

Let's look at the example of Rebecca Clever. Rebecca wants to apply for a weekend job to get some money together to help her with driving lessons. She also thinks by getting some employment this will help her when she comes to leave school. She is interested in working with animals eventually and decides to try to get some employment at one of the local pet shops in the area.

Rebecca hasn't written a CV before so she gets her CV done for her by her mum. Rebecca sends off the following cover letter and attached CV to a local pet shop owner.

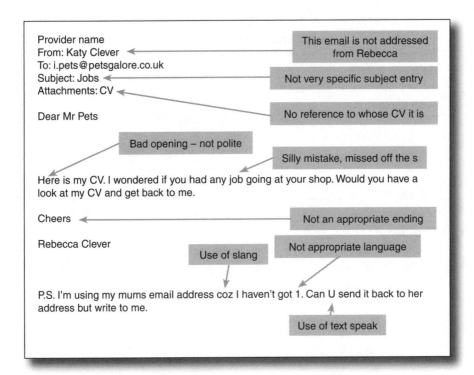

The owner of Pets Galore, Mr Pets is scratching his head. He feels he doesn't know Rebecca at all and doesn't understand the cover letter. He notices the following things about the cover letter and email cover letter she has sent him.

- It isn't so much a cover letter as a cover note. It doesn't seem to tell him anything and he can't even reply to Rebecca directly, only through her mother. He doesn't know what sort of job she is looking for, part-time, full-time or whether she lives locally.
- He notices there is no introduction to herself or to him. She hasn't labelled her CV by name and hasn't put a specific enough reference to the email.
- He also notices she has put job instead of jobs.
- He notices that Rebecca uses text speak for the P.S. comments and doesn't even bother to spell out the words **one**, **because** or **you** fully. He also notices that she has missed the apostrophe on mums.

He decides (against his better judgement) to open the CV to find out some more and make the situation clearer.

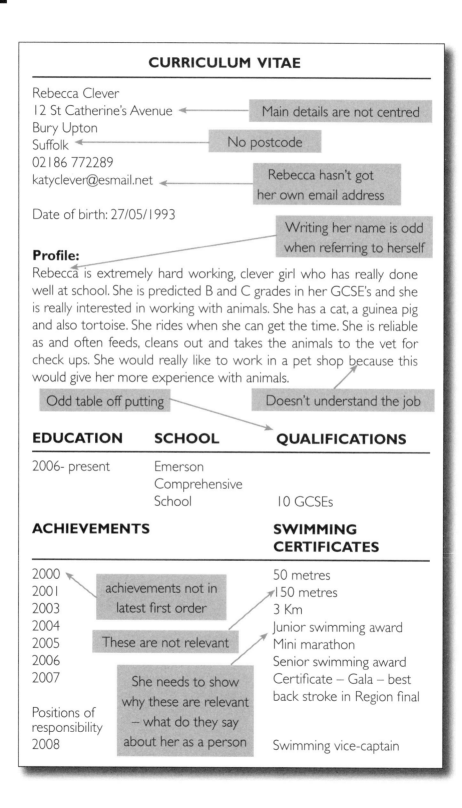

CURRICULUM VITAE

Rebecca Clever
12 St Catherine's Avenue ←——— Main details are not centred
Bury Upton
Suffolk ←——————— No postcode
02186 772289
katyclever@esmail.net ←——— Rebecca hasn't got her own email address

Date of birth: 27/05/1993

Writing her name is odd when referring to herself

Profile:
Rebecca is extremely hard working, clever girl who has really done well at school. She is predicted B and C grades in her GCSE's and she is really interested in working with animals. She has a cat, a guinea pig and also tortoise. She rides when she can get the time. She is reliable as and often feeds, cleans out and takes the animals to the vet for check ups. She would really like to work in a pet shop because this would give her more experience with animals.

Odd table off putting

Doesn't understand the job

EDUCATION	SCHOOL	QUALIFICATIONS
2006- present	Emerson Comprehensive School	10 GCSEs

ACHIEVEMENTS	SWIMMING CERTIFICATES
2000	50 metres
2001	150 metres
2003	3 Km
2004	Junior swimming award
2005	Mini marathon
2006	Senior swimming award
2007	Certificate – Gala – best back stroke in Region final
Positions of responsibility	
2008	Swimming vice-captain

achievements not in latest first order

These are not relevant

She needs to show why these are relevant – what do they say about her as a person

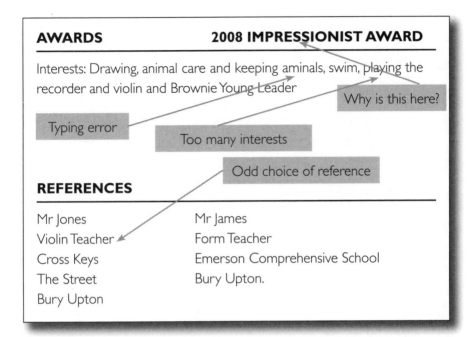

The CV

- The first thing he notices is that the layout of the CV is very strange. The main personal details are not centred, and there is no postcode. There is a strange box that has been put in for education but which makes the CV difficult to read.

- Another thing that strikes Mr Pets is that the CV isn't written by Rebecca. He thinks this because she has written the profile in the third person inserting her own name. He also notes that the email address is not Rebecca's but her mum, Katy's.

- The profile does mention her interest and some skills in care for animals. However, looking after the pets is only one thing about the job. Most of the time in the shop staff deal with customers, take money and sell animal products. He can't see any skills she has that relate to this.

- The profile also is littered with grammatical errors, such as the apostrophe in GCSEs and the missing 'an' in the first sentence.

- The achievements seem to be around swimming and art – not animals or relevant areas.

- Positions of responsibility show that Rebecca has done well at Brownies but doesn't say what this achievement means. She has also won an art competition, but again this doesn't seem relevant.
- There is no mention of other types of employment or work experience.
- Interests are merely listed and there are so many. Rebecca hasn't put down enough about her interest in animals to make this stand out to him.
- There is a typing error in the last sentence where she has put aminals instead of animals.
- One of the references is an odd choice of her violin teacher. None of the references are complete. They do not have postcodes on them or telephone or email details.

Rebecca doesn't hear anything and begins to wonder if she hasn't done the cover letter and CV right. She shows her careers co-ordinator at her school. After talking to her she is much clearer.

A good CV and cover letter

Rebecca decides to send off an improved cover letter and CV to another local pet shop. First she rings up the pet shop owner and asks to speak to him. He says he hasn't got a vacancy currently but if she sends in her CV and cover letter he will consider her for a job if anyone leaves or goes part-time. After gaining some ideas about what working at Happy Pets is like she writes the following cover letter which she attaches with her new CV also.

Provider name

From: rebecca.clever@e.mail.com — Rebecca has email address for reply

To: JohnParrot@vhappypets.co.uk

Subject: Saturday Work — Better subject heading

Attachments: CV Rebecca Clever

Dear Mr Parrot — Good use of 'hook' refers to previous contact

Following our telephone conversation yesterday I am writing to confirm my interest in possible future Saturday work at Happy Pets.

I am looking to work eventually in a career with animals but feel I need to gain some real employment experience in other areas such as retail. I am only available on Saturdays presently due to being at school full-time and my other commitments in my free time with swimming and Brownies. I do live locally to the shop in St Catherine's Avenue.

Rebecca tells him when she can work

Rebecca shows how close she lives to the employer

I have lots of skills to offer as you will see from my attached CV. I have excellent verbal and written communication skills and have customer service experience from my work experience at Bury Upton Library. I also have been on a till before, and can work out basic money calculations well. I am organised, reliable and hardworking as my experience both in my swimming and Brownies shows. I am also resourceful as is shown in my art award.

Rebecca has made her previous experience and skills relevant to this job

I would really like to work for Happy Pets as it is an excellent store and I have visited it for my own pets. I feel it would give me valuable employment experience which I could take on to a course or apprenticeship once I leave school.

I know that at present you have no vacancies, but I hope you will keep my CV on file. Please contact me either by email or phone if any suitable vacancies arise.

Yours sincerely,   Appropriate ending

Rebecca Clever

Nice personal touch

Attach: CV

- Mr Parrot is impressed. He likes the way Rebecca has laid out the email as if it was a letter and when he prints it off, it looks good on paper as well. It is clearly laid out and refers to his telephone conversation with Rebecca that he now remembers.

- One crucial thing he notes is that she lives locally and he knows St Catherine's Avenue as it is two streets away.

- He also likes the fact that Rebecca has made clear what she can do and what she can't as this helps him think about his present staffing at the shop.

- She has lots of relevant skills to offer him and he is pleased she has chosen carefully to highlight the skills most needed for this position.

- He likes also that she has mentioned the shop, and has been into it as a customer. He thinks this shows a personal interest and touch.

He also feels that she could be useful in the future even if she does go on to an apprenticeship or college as she might want to stay working for him part-time.

He looks at the letter and notes she has referred to her CV. He now opens the attached CV to see the points she has mentioned.

REBECCA CLEVER

12 St Catherine's Avenue, Bury Upton, Suffolk, IX22 3RX
Tel: 02186 772289
Mobile: 00078790385
Email: rebecca.clever@e.mail.com

Clear layout

PERSONAL PROFILE:

I am a hardworking, self-motivated young person with a real passion for caring for animals. I am looking for a Saturday job which will combine my interest in animals with gaining experience of work. I am physically fit and used to getting up early for swimming. I am a reliable and trustworthy team member. I would enjoy being able to gain more skills and learn more about customer service in the retail environment.

Rebecca has chosen carefully which skills to highlight

Well targeted personal statement

KEY SKILLS:

- Small animal care from my own pets including experience of cleaning, feeding, and medical care when needed after vet visits.
- Excellent communication skills both verbal and written.
- Good numerical skills including ability to add up figures and work out percentages.
- Leadership and organisation skills. I have the ability to receive instructions well and also take responsibility when asked to do so. This is shown in my Young Leader role.

EDUCATION HISTORY:

2004-present	**Emerson Comprehensive School, Bury Upton**
	Currently in Year 11 studying 10 GCSEs including Maths, English, Double Science. Predicted grade Science BB.

Rebecca has chosen to show the grades most of interest

Achievements:	**Impressionist Artists Award – Emerson School**
	I won this award last year. The picture I painted was a painting of "Cows in a field" done in the impressionist style of Kandinsky. This involved researching the artist and his works.

Rebecca shows how this is relevant – showing she had to do research

WORK EXPERIENCE: BURY UPTON LIBRARY

I spent two weeks in Year 10 at the main library in Bury Upton. This involved helping customers with enquiries both face to face and on the phone. I also used the library IT system to keep client records of loans, payments and reservations. I took payments and operated the till under supervision. As part of the experience I was responsible for organising a display in the central foyer on children's favourite stories.

Rebecca makes the work experience relevant showing customer service skills, till work, and organising displays.

VOLUNTARY WORK:

I am a Young Leader at First St Catherine's Brownies. This involves looking after and instructing Brownies aged 7–11 years of age. I also help the Brownies with their badges and I assisted with the activities recently on the Friends to Animals badge, including how to care for pets and a visit to a local animal charity.

Rebecca relates her voluntary work to pets

I also help out sometimes with publicising local charity swimming events, including distributing leaflets around school and in the community.

INTERESTS:

Animals: I have two pet cats, a guinea pig and a tortoise. I care for my animals every day with feeding, cleaning out and also taking to the vets or giving medicines when needed. I also ride well and visit the St Catherine's riding club weekly.

Swimming: I swim three times a week and practice for mini marathons and galas with the Dolphins Swimming Club.

Rebecca's chooses just two of interests but gives details of both

REFERENCES:

Mr Paul James	Mrs S Watts
Form Tutor	Brown Owl
Year 11	First St Catherine's Brownies
Emerson Comprehensive School	22 St Catherine's Street
Bury Upton	Bury Upton
IP22 4TX	IP22 7TB
Tel: 02186 3333 Ext 72	Tel: 02186 778811
Email: p.james@emerson-school.org.	Email: s.watts@emailtr.co.uk

References are well chosen and complete with postcodes and contact details

- Mr Parrott is immediately struck by the easy to read layout of the CV. He can see clearly from her personal statement what she is looking for and has to offer him. He likes the fact she can get up in the morning for swimming as he once had a young person working for him before who never made it to the shop on time. He remembers mentioning this to her on the phone and she has obviously picked this up.
- The skills she has chosen really match what he is looking for in the shop as he needs people who can talk to customers and also work out percentages as there are often discounts in the shop. She has some experience of animal care and he likes the fact she volunteers with the Brownies. He thinks she may know many of the parents and customers coming into the shop and this is an advantage.
- His overall impression of the CV is that Rebecca has really made her CV complement her cover letter. He feels she has put in hard work and gone to some extra effort to highlight her skills in relation to what he needs in the shop. He thinks hard about his staffing rota and knows that in a few months' time one of his members of staff is looking to go part-time. He thinks Rebecca might be just the person to fill this gap.

Rebecca is pleased to receive a reply from Mr Parrot a week later saying he will definitely consider her for future vacancies.

If Rebecca wanted to try for some other vacancies, but these were, for example, with horses, then she would have to write a new cover letter but could adapt her present CV to the new opportunities. She would do this by changing the information in the personal profile of the CV to be more about her interest in horses and altering her skills and interests to be more about what she had gained from being with horses.

Important points to remember for your CV and cover letter

Always tailor your cover letter and CV

This is the most important thing to remember when sending a cover letter with a CV. Make sure that each are tailored to the position or company you are applying for. Follow any application guidelines you may have been given to the letter and take the time to make sure they work well together. It does mean a new letter for each new opportunity and adapting a CV to fit with the letter and the new opportunity also although you do not in most cases have to start from scratch again with your CV.

Attachments – are they there?

It is tempting when sending off a cover letter by email to attach the CV at the end. This often leads to CVs never getting attached. It is worth attaching the CV *first* before writing the cover letter if this is written in the text of the email. Always make sure your attachments are clearly labelled. If you are applying for more than one vacancy check and double check you have sent the correct CV with the right cover letter!

Mention the CV in the letter

Although you don't want to repeat information from the cover letter you should mention there is a CV attached or enclosed.

Always write your cover letter and CV yourself

There are lots of services available now to get other people and professions to write your cover letter or CV for you. Getting professional advice on how to write a good cover letter and CV is fine but it is not a good idea to get someone else to do it for you, otherwise it is likely to cause problems later on. It also is unlikely to come across as genuinely you – this is what the employer wants to see.

Keep cover letters and CVs to the right length

The general guidelines are one side of A4 for a cover letter and no more. If it is an email try to make the letter easy to read on screen and maybe a little shorter. For CVs no more than two sides of A4.

Always use appropriate language and keep things simple

It is important that you do not refer to yourself in the third person by name, for example like Rebecca did. If you want to write your personal statement in the third person, as is still suggested sometimes, then simply miss out the 'I', for example 'a first year undergraduate'. Make sure all language is appropriate and do not abbreviate terms in either the CV or cover letter except for titles i.e. Dr. It is better to keep formatting and layout simple so that it is easy to read.

Always present your cover letter and CV in the best condition

This sounds like an obvious thing to say. However, it is quite common for applicants to turn up with a cover letter and CV in a shabby folder and looking the worse for wear. One recruitment consultant gave me these tips.

> 'If you are going to go to the bother of doing a really good cover letter and CV then make sure you put it into a nice plastic or waterproof folder so that when we get to see it, it looks good. Another thing is to never put it at the bottom of a shopping bag – it never comes out the same as it went in.'

A cover letter and CV are the perfect match for one another and once you get a good example of both you can then learn and adapt this to make every cover letter and CV a winning combination.

7

Cover letters/emails to go with application forms

Cover letters that go with application forms are nearly always directed at a specific job vacancy or opportunity. The application form is designed and set by the employer and so the employer will be getting the same type of information from all applicants.

This chapter will look in detail at:

- following the application carefully to ensure your cover letter is accurate and mentions everything the application asks for
- how to write a good supporting statement
- sending your cover letter for an application as an email.

In this situation you are limited, apart from in the personal statement of an application form, as to the impact you can have on the employer. Your cover letter therefore becomes crucial in this case to show who you really are and how you differ from other candidates.

Some companies or application schemes now want an online application form filled out and may not request a cover letter in this instance. Companies that do this often ask you to go to their own website. This will be tailormade to the company and you must do this carefully as this will then be the first time an employer has made contact with you. It is also wise to print off what you have written so you know when you come to interview what exactly you have said.

TIP Take some time before filling in the online form to look at the website in general and really understand what the company is looking for. This will make targeting your application easier.

Another example of an online application scheme, where an online form is filled out, is for the online application for apprenticeships. This form is filled out just once and then the details are matched to vacancies the person is looking for. For more details on applying for apprenticeships this way go to www.apprenticeships.org.uk.

Despite these other ways of applying many companies or organisations will want an application emailed or sent by post with a cover letter accompanying it. This is to your advantage as you can really make a good first impression and show something uniquely attractive about yourself to the employer.

Just like with CVs, your cover letter for an application form has to be of a very high standard and also must complement the application form, particularly pulling out one or two specific items that are mentioned in the job vacancy or job specification. These points should have been covered in the supporting statement of the form. The letter gives you the chance to point to these aspects and says to the employer – read my application.

Let's look at an example of Philip Readymeal. Philip has been checking out his local Connexions website vacancy service. He looks every week at all the vacancies on Help You Get There and sees one this week he likes the look of. He reads the following vacancy details.

CATERING ASSISTANT VACANCY REF: 1782

Type: Employment
Hours: 40 hours per week
Minimum Qualifications: No qualifications needed
Wage: 16/17 years £3.53 ph, 18/19 yrs 4.77 ph to start
Location: Hunston by the Sea

Details: This is an excellent opportunity to learn all aspects of the catering business. You will start by learning how to prepare vegetables and salads and will then progress, learning how to cook the full range of dishes on the menu. This will include home made soups, sauces, cottage pies, lasagne, curries etc. Other duties will include learning how to use the griddle to cook steaks, burgers etc, washing up and keeping the kitchen area clean and tidy.

To apply: Please contact Julie Bold at Connexions on 08156 774466 to request an application form and further details of the application.

Philip rings Julie and finds out that he has to complete an application form and also that he has to do a cover letter to the employer. Julie sends him the form, a job description and job specification through the post from the employer.

A bad example of a cover letter

Philip notes the following from the job specifications.

Job specifications: Vacancy Ref: 178235

Qualifications and qualities: No qualifications are required for this position.

We are looking for a hard working individual who has a genuine interest in working in the catering industry. The ability to take pride in your work, pay attention to detail and be able to work under pressure is essential. Good communication skills and enthusiasm are also key requirements.

Previous experience in a food related industry is not required but ability to work well in a team is important.

Hours: 40 hours per week working 5 days out of 7 on a rota. 8 hour days, split shifts between the hours of 10 a.m. and 10 p.m. – to be discussed at the interview.

Training: In-house training given. There will also be the possibility of day release/training towards an NVQ level 2 in Food Preparation.

Other information: This vacancy would suit someone who has a keen interest in catering and who is looking for a career in catering.

To apply: Please complete a *Connexions application form* and send with a cover letter by post to Mrs Elaine Jolly at the employer's address given below.

Deadline for applications: Friday 8 May 2009

Name of Contact: Mrs Elaine Jolly

Position: Restaurant Manager
Tel: 08485 7119900
Web: www.theseasidecabin.co.uk

Company Name: The Seaside Cabin
Company Address: 17 North Parade, Hunston by the Sea, Norfolk, PE31 2SL

Philip looks at the job specifications and then leaves it for another week. He then remembers the deadline for the application was this Friday and it is now Thursday. He hasn't got long so he quickly fills in the application form and sends the following cover letter.

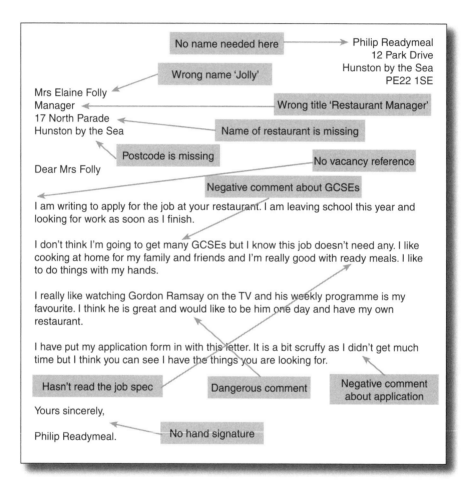

- Philip has really let himself down here in this letter. He has rushed it and made lots of silly mistakes. The first thing Mrs Jolly notices is he has actually got her name wrong, and hasn't put the name of the restaurant. This is not a good start.
- He has pointed out lots of negatives about his application and drawn attention to his lack of GCSEs – which is not a good thing.

- He also mentions he likes Gordon Ramsay. This is a dangerous game to play because he doesn't know that the manager will agree with him on this and if she doesn't it could work against him.
- Philip hasn't related anything in his letter except for the lack of his GCSEs to the job specifications. In particular he hasn't noted the emphasis on home cooked food. Being good with ready meals is not what Mrs Jolly is looking for.
- He also mentions his application form, but not in a good way, and doesn't bring out the points in the application form he wants the employer to look at.

On Friday that week Mrs Jolly is sitting in her restaurant at the end of a busy day looking through all the applications that have now come in.

She looks through about 25 applications in total. She is tired and rather disappointed at most of them. There is one however from Henry Salt that really stands out.

A good example of a cover letter

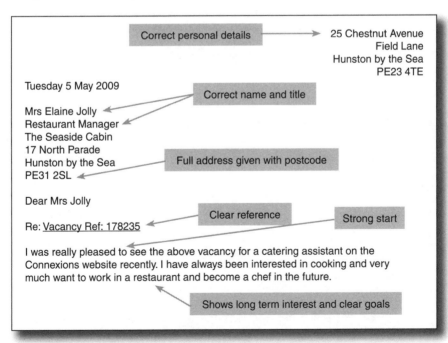

My interest in cooking started a few years ago when I stayed with my aunt over the summer holidays. She is a fantastic cook and showed me how to do the basics. I now cook for the family and sometimes my friends. My signature dish is baked fish and spinach with a tarragon and garlic dressing. I get the fish fresh from a local fishmonger.

Demonstrates experience   Shows long standing interest

As you will see from my application form, I am hard working and used to working under time pressure. I have had a paper round for the last two years which means working in all conditions and getting the papers out on time for customers. This has also meant getting up early in the mornings.

Refers to application form positively
and points out strengths

I am looking to leave school this summer and get an apprenticeship which will allow me to train on the job. I have dyslexia which does sometimes mean I have to check spellings of words and numbers. With a school tutor, I have been able to work around these problems in a practical way and now am much more confident.

Shows good attitude to disability

I notice from your website that your restaurant specialises in cooking fresh fish. I would love to be able to develop the skills I already have in the kitchen and produce other fish dishes. Cooking fish is a real passion and this opportunity seems perfect for me.

Has done research

I hope you will consider my application. My exams are during May and June but not every day so I could attend an interview at the weekends or when I'm not sitting an exam. I really look forward to being able to meet you and see your restaurant soon.

Best Wishes
Yours sincerely,   Tells the employer when he is free

Harry Salt

Harry Salt
Enc × 1

- She is really impressed by Henry's application. He has really gone the extra mile. She notes that he has bothered to go onto the website to find out more about the Seaside Cabin.

- He has got all the basic details correct and has put the address in full. He has put the reference of the job for which he is applying to make it easier for her. She likes the fact his letter comes on fresh clean white paper and the envelope has been carefully addressed.

- He hasn't made any mistakes in his letter and has obviously checked the letter or got it checked. He comes across as enthusiastic and keen to learn. She likes the fact that he isn't afraid of hard work and has done a paper round for several years.
- She looks at the points he has raised about his application form. She turns to his application form to see the pieces in it he has referred to. She is impressed by how carefully typed the application is, particularly considering she knows he has dyslexia. She thinks Henry has taken time and effort over the application. She looks at his personal statement.

Personal Statement/Comments to support your application
(include personal characteristics; skills and tasks during work experience, part-time jobs, voluntary work and other skills or abilities — look at the job description and match your experience to the tasks listed)

I am a hard working pupil in Year 11 at Hunston by the Sea High School and looking for my first job after leaving school. I really would like to work in a restaurant and learn how to cook properly as cooking is my main passion at home. My favourite subject at school is Domestic Science.

I have had a paper round for two years, which I have never missed or been late for. I am very reliable and enjoy making sure the job gets done properly. I have many disabled customers on my rounds who I know personally and take extra care to cater for their needs.

On work experience in Year 10, I went to a local baker's selling food called 'Oven Delights'. I learnt how to get the cakes and bread baked in time for the customers and to plan the days baking. I served customers under supervision, and took lunch orders on the phone from local businesses. I really loved preparing the lunch orders especially the 'to order' made salads.

My main speciality is cooking fresh local fish. I often cook for my family. I also am good at puddings and most enjoy making toffee cream pudding. I do this with a coconut sauce which is delicious. The most important thing for me about cooking is to see a beautiful meal produced at the end having started out with just raw produce. I love seeing people happy with my food.

I would love the chance to do an apprenticeship. I really enjoy cooking and I have learnt a lot about health and safety of food in my GCSE in Domestic Science.

For me working in a sea food restaurant would be the beginning of my dream.

Signed: *Harry Salt*

Date: 5 May 2009

Mrs Jolly feels she has formed a fairly accurate picture of Henry from his letter and application form. He comes across to her as extremely caring, hard working and really wanting to work in catering. She can see his enthusiasm for food just leaping off the page.

She notes that he has some needs but feels that his willingness and good attitude can overcome any difficulties he may have. She feels he is a doer with a good attitude to others who will be an asset in her restaurant.

She has no doubt in offering him an interview. A week later Henry hears he has got the job.

The moral of the story

What this shows is that at the end of the day enthusiasm, the right attitude, care and attention to the employer's needs really pay off. These can be far more important to an employer than lots of qualifications from someone who doesn't care or isn't interested in what they do. Both the letter and the application form have to show you care and you care more than the other applicants.

A few tips about completing application forms

Although this isn't a book about application forms, the importance of doing an application form well is obvious, as without this your winning cover letter is wasted.

Here are a few tips to remember.

- Read the instructions that come with the form. Follow them to the letter. If it says fill in block capitals or black ink then you must do just that.
- Match your skills, qualifications and qualities as closely as possible to those given in the application. Give examples to demonstrate them in practice.
- If you are sending the application form with a cover letter do the application form first. This is because the specifications you are trying to match will be included in your supporting statement section of the form. You can then pick out a few of your best skills or qualities to highlight in the letter. Then both the application form and letter will complement each other.
- Use the same font for both if they are both typed.
- Always photocopy (more than once if necessary) the form if you can or scan it before you write or type on it so you can have another go if you mess up.
- Applications take time, so make sure you leave plenty of time, say over a weekend, to complete one. They often take more time than you think. Give yourself time to check the form twice to make sure you haven't made obvious mistakes. Get someone else to check it.
- If you are listing any qualifications or work experience/employment on the form remember it is just like a CV, the latest comes first. Don't mix and match, stick to this throughout the form.
- Use a dictionary if you don't know how to spell something. Don't guess, and watch casual language or clichés in the supporting statement.
- Lastly and probably the most important thing. Fill in every part of the form that you are required to. If you leave anything undone or the form is not signed you have lost before you have started.

Cutting and pasting the supporting statement

One of the most difficult aspects of any application form is how to get the main statement to look good. If you risk writing it and if your handwriting isn't neat and you don't practice beforehand you can make a mess of it. You can run out of room or make errors which can't be easily corrected. Unless you are very good with correcting fluid this probably isn't an option.

The best way is to type the supporting statements. However, this also takes time. You can opt to type it in a Word document and then physically cut and paste onto a form. This can work well if you have received the application form by post and you haven't got the skill needed to put the form through your printer.

The other way is to copy the document and then paste it electronically onto the right section of the form. This is easy if the form has been emailed to you but if it has been sent through the post this can be a challenge and may take several attempts – so photocopy the form several times BEFORE you attempt to do this.

Sending an emailed cover letter for a placement application

Lets look at an example of an emailed cover letter that goes with an application.

Simon Tang is a second year undergraduate at Smithfield University. He is studying computer and communication systems engineering. As part of the course there is a year out in industry and students are encouraged by the placement officer to help find a suitable placement which best suits their interests and areas of study.

English is not his first language although he has lived in the UK now for several years. He knows he has to be careful about how he phrases his English as sometimes he doesn't get this quite right.

Simon has found a company in Birmingham that he is really interested in applying to. He has looked on their website and noticed they are asking for a cover letter and application form to be sent back by email to them.

He is excited by the company because they offer a wide range of placement experience and most importantly going to this company will help him gain his Certificate in Industrial Studies as part of his degree. He knows however the company will probably get lots of letters from students similar to himself so he really has to make his letter stand out.

To: Susan.taylor@btisystems.co.uk
From: simon.tang@e-mailsmtihfielduni.ac.uk
CC:
Subject: Industrial Placement IP/SA1/09

Clear reference

Good hook

Dear Ms Taylor *He is unsure if she is Mrs/Miss so he puts Ms*

I am presently an undergraduate in the second year of a degree in Computer and Communication Systems Engineering at Smithfield University. I remember seeing you come to the Engineering show last year on campus and was really impressed by your Industrial Placement Programme which I discussed with one of your colleagues.

Good reasons for picking this company

I am looking for a chance to spend a year in industry and am particularly interested in your scheme because of the variety of placement experience it offers. It also offers me the opportunity to obtain my Certificate in Industrial Studies which I really want to achieve during the placement period.

As you will see from my application I have performed well on my course and obtained a first in two of the modules this year. I also have the advantage of speaking two other languages, standard Mandarin and Cantonese. These can be advantageous languages when working abroad particularly in South East Asia. I notice your company has a base in Singapore.

Simon shows his unique skills

During my time at university I have also worked part-time locally in a computer retailer. This has helped me improve my customer relation skills and liaison with suppliers. I am also the vice-president this year of Chinese Soc and help produce its termly newsletter distributed on campus. This has involved planning and working with a team for editing and distribution.

This helps show his life skills

I am aware of the international reputation of BTI systems as one of the world's leading authorities on telecommunications. I particularly noted in February's *Communications Weekly* the launch of the company's new fibre optics systems. I would love the chance to work in such a dynamic company, and one which will form a foundation to my future career in systems engineering.

Excellent research

I look forward to hearing from you soon. I can be contacted on my mobile 08112 763913 or via email.

Yours sincerely
Simon Tang

Susan Taylor is a very busy human resources officer at BTI systems looking through over 200 applications for five places. She particularly like Simon's cover letter. It stands out to her for the following reasons.

- He has already made the effort to find out about the company before he has written. He mentions seeing her at the Engineering show and now she does recall seeing Simon.
- She thinks he has chosen good reasons for picking the placement and has done his research in what it offers.
- She is impressed by his level of skills. He has highlighted his unique selling points that other candidates don't have, for example his first in two modules and also the fact that he speaks two other languages. This is really of interest to her as the company has a base in Singapore and this might be relevant if they liked him on the placement and wanted to take him on after his degree.
- He has gained general life skills. He has held down a job part-time and also been involved in a university society. He has shown her exactly what these experiences have taught him – she likes this.
- The thing that really clinches it for Susan is Simon's last paragraph. She knows from reading this he is interested in his subject and communications as he is reading the relevant journals. She is impressed that he knows about the launch of their new system and this is something that no other candidate has noticed.
- Susan's impression of Simon is that he is genuinely interested in his degree subject and the company. He seems sound and well rounded, with unique skills but not boastful. She looks at his application, which is neat, and where he expands on many of the skills he has. She decides to offer him an interview there and then as she wants to meet him again.

In both the successful letters above the winning formula is based upon an impression they create in the mind of the employer. If it is positive they will go on to read the application and more than this you will already have a 'halo' effect when they do so. As long as your form then delivers a similar message you are on the way to the Yes pile.

If you have a letter to write, read it back to yourself from an employer's view. How do you come across, what messages have you sent to the employer? It is not just what you write, but critically the overall picture that you create.

8

Top ten tips for winning cover letters

During the research for this book, I had many of the same or similar comments made by employers, work based learning providers, recruiters, personal advisers and agency staff. Here are some of their comments I have compiled to give you the top ten tips for that winning cover letter.

Number 10

Make sure you know what you are applying for

This sounds too obvious, doesn't it? Many of the employers I saw complained that candidates often hadn't read the job descriptions or lists of duties and some just had got the job completely wrong.

> 'Further to our conversation on the phone I would like to apply for the position in television sales'

The position was for telesales.

One employer stated:

> 'I've had it all. Too often clients don't read the job specs properly. I've even had a client who thought personal assistant was some kind of personal shopper!'

On the positive side some applicants are able to demonstrate they 'get' it

'I am a recent graduate applying for the position of trainee journalist. I have undertaken work experience during my journalism course at a number of national press agencies and regional newspapers.'

Number 9

Always write a professional letter

Some examples of letters were sent on bits of paper, different coloured paper, emails with text abbreviations in them, and quick one line emails. One employer made the following comment.

'The best example I have ever seen of what not to do was when I received a letter from someone who had handwritten a letter on the back of another document – it was unbelievable really.'

Never use text abbreviations in emails.

'Can U send me plse the details of the job you have going in the store. I want to apply for it.

Thanx'

One employer commented:

'I once received a letter sent by post – some would consider old fashioned – with her CV attached. The letter was written in the neatest handwriting I had ever seen, the paper was high quality, and her CV was perfect, even the envelope was white and clean. It was beautiful and she had taken great pride in sending this to me. I can still remember that application to this day.'

Number 8

Show that you are really enthusiastic about the job

All the agencies I spoke to and some personal advisers had come across candidates applying for jobs they clearly were not interested in and didn't understand why they had applied. One employer said:

> 'Some applicants just don't get it. They waffle on about their experience and qualifications. What I want to know is do they actually want the job. Where is their enthusiasm? What about the job interests them?'

A typical example was:

> 'I am out of work right now and need to find a job. I have been advised to apply for this position.'

However, all had also had some brilliant letters from applicants whose enthusiasm made them interview them.

> 'I have enjoyed being around animals ever since childhood and I would be able to bring lots of enthusiasm and commitment to your company'

This young person was taken on as a result of her cover letter.

Number 7

Tailor your cover letter to the employer or position

> 'I understand that the RSPCA is one of the largest charities for re-housing all types of animals and I would love to be a part of that.'

This young person also gained the placement he wanted.

> 'I have an interest in electrical maintenance through working with my Dad and a friend. I also have experience of working on and off site with electrical equipment. I am a very hands on person'

This young person was taken on for an electrical apprenticeship.

Number 6

Research the company

Many employers commented that applicants didn't research enough into their company.

> 'We get loads of applicants for our positions and it is always clear which ones really know what we do and have bothered to find out what we offer.'

Some good examples were:

> 'I am interested in First Choice Travel because of its position as one of the UK's leading travel companies and a member of the Association of British Travel Agents.'

> 'I understand your company deals with a wide range of design aspects such as web design, graphics and digital print. I feel I would fit comfortably in your business.'

Number 5

Always attach or enclose relevant documents

There are two problems that employers and agencies stated with this. Some applicants just forgot and others attached the wrong documents. One employer stated:

'I had a situation once where we were recruiting for a number of positions in advertising sales. One applicant actually attached his application for a rival advertising group – disaster. You wouldn't want him putting in the births, deaths and marriages would you.'

Another said:

'I get quite tired of seeing applicants say 'see attached CV' and there isn't anything. Why don't they check?'

On the plus side someone always gets it right

'We had an advert once that had quite a lot of different parts to it. We got all sorts of problems as applicants didn't read what was needed and didn't send half of the parts back. However, just two got it right – we interviewed those two.'

Number 4

Sell your positives, don't mention the negatives

All agencies and employers stated that mentioning negative information in an application put them off.

'Although I do not have a qualification in accounting or any experience of accounts my general experience in administration has helped me acquire relevant office skills.'

This candidate didn't need to emphasise what they don't have and can't do. Similarly,

'I undertook a NVQ level 1 in Vehicle Maintenance which I really enjoyed doing but due to a school change I was unable to complete the course.'

This may be very valid but gives out a negative vibe. This would have been positive if he had just said about the course and what he enjoyed on it at the time.

'I did a work placement while I was on the course where I worked with both feral and house cats which included feeding and cleaning of the cats.'

This applicant showed what they had achieved and enjoyed.

Number 3

Keep it short and simple in layout and style

Writing too much or not using short sentences was mentioned by many employers and recruitment agencies.

'Lots of applicants, particularly those who are at college or university, seem to write their personal statements like an essay. They go on and on. They don't realise that in this business I haven't got time to spend that amount of time on each application.'

However, in some cases there was a worry about young people in particular not putting enough detail and effort into their letters.

'Obviously you don't want lots of unnecessary details but I find many young people we see here don't give enough information about what they enjoy and want to do. Sometimes you get one line and that is it. The best thing is to see a few short well structured paragraphs so that there is some relevant information which is easy to read.'

Number 2

Always read the instructions

This was mentioned by employers as one of the most common and most annoying mistakes. They stated that most of the applicants didn't read instructions carefully enough.

'On our application form the main details are meant to be in block capital letters. About half that come back don't fill this bit in correctly. These have blown it straightaway.'

One employer stated:

'When you get one that has followed the instructions they stand out. You can see them straightaway.'

Number 1

Make sure the information is truthful and correct. No mistakes

'The worse crime I think is when the person can't spell your name right. It is so annoying when you get letters that are not addressed properly even if my name is difficult to spell. It is always on the vacancy details but lots of applicants can't be bothered.'

Some other examples were:

'I once had someone apply for a position as a Chief. Of course she meant Chef!'

'I done work experience at my dads firm. I found it very intresting. I believe I have the nessary skill to benefit the company and what the job involves.'

You can see there are many errors including 'done' instead of 'did', wrong spellings and no apostrophe for dad's.

However, if you do make the extra effort to check your cover letter it may be the only one that is right and that gives you the chance to be the winning applicant.

'Cover letters in my opinion are never checked enough. Very rarely do you get one without any errors, but when you do it is usually worth reading.'

9

Winning cover letters – final thoughts to take away

Hopefully what you have gained from this book is some basic guidelines and a good understanding of what makes a Winning Cover Letter.

Cover letters will always differ in style and content because every individual is different. You should write a winning cover letter that follows the right format, style and basic rules but still doesn't lose 'you' as a person. If you remember one thing from reading this book, then remember this.

The employer wants to employ a genuine, enthusiastic and unique individual. They will want to see that you have relevant skills, qualities and experience but they also want to employ you as a person. They want to know you are interested and care about what they do.

In return you want to be employed in a company that will allow you to develop yourself and perhaps lead you nearer to your dreams. A humble cover letter can do just that. It might be that you are writing a letter to gain your very first job, a part-time job, or undertake voluntary work. From these beginnings can come a fulfilling and long lasting career.

I once spoke to someone who applied to a newspaper for work in the summer when she was a student at university. After graduating she couldn't find a graduate job so she went back to the newspaper to help them out in her old job. Twenty years later she heads up the design studio of the same newspaper and loves her job. It all started with a single cover letter and CV.

If you care about every cover letter you write as if it holds the beginnings of your dreams then you will be on the right track to making that cover letter the winning one.

10
Resources and information

Advice on employment law and equal opportunities

ACAS: www.acas.org.uk
ACAS has a telephone helpline for legal enquiries Tel: 08457 474747.

Citizens Advice Bureau: www.citizensadvice.org.uk
Your local CAB office will be in the local phone directory.

Careers advice links

Young people 13–19 years

Connexions: www.connexions-direct.com
Connexions is a young people's service that can help with a range of issues including apprenticeships, careers and funding advice. Your local Connexions office can be found by going onto this site and looking under local services.

Useful publications: Connexions services produce their own local guides to training and job opportunities in their area. Contact your local Connexions offices to ask about these.

Graduates

Prospects: www.prospects.ac.uk
This is the official UK graduate website and contains advice, information and vacancy information for graduates.

Useful publication: *Prospects Directory: The A–Z of Graduate Jobs and Training* is a publication guide to help graduates find employers and gives advice and tips on how to apply.

Adults

http://careersadvice.direct.gov.uk
Information on training and careers for adults

Next Step: www.direct.gov.uk
This site provides information on all the Next Step services in the UK. They offer information, advice and guidance to adults on learning, careers and job hunting in the UK. You can find your local Next Step office by going onto this site. Look under Adult Learning and Skills for face to face advice.

Apprenticeships

Apprenticeships: www.apprenticeships.org.uk
This site contains all the information about apprenticeships in the UK including the Apprenticeship Vacancy Matching Service.

Apprenticeship hotline 08000 150 600
You can ring this hotline to find out more about apprenticeships and get information sent to you.

Useful publication: *The Apprenticeship Guide* also available online at www.apprenticeshipguide.co.uk
This contains information on what is an apprenticeship, lists learning providers in the UK by region, and lists types of apprenticeships.

Job search and information sites

Careers Box: www.careersbox.co.uk
This gives free access to film about careers and courses. It contains case studies on film of real people doing real jobs. This can be useful to get information about a job or career area.

Careerbuilder: www.careerbuilder.co.uk

This site offers job vacancy information, tips on cover letters, CVs and interviews.

Jobs4U: Available on the Connexions Direct website www.connexions-direct.com/Jobs4U

This offers a good careers information database.

Local papers: Local papers will often have an online job vacancy section which will give you all the jobs in your direct local area. Contact your local paper for details.

Monster: www.monster.co.uk

This is a typical job search site but has information about applying, including cover letters.

Resources to help with writing skills

Oxford English Dictionary: www.askoxford.com

This is a free online site that uses the *Compact Oxford English Dictionary* to search for correct spellings.

Skillswise: www.bbc.co.uk/skillswise

This site gives simple but effective advice on the use of English including writing skills, grammar, punctuation and even vocabulary which is linked to career areas.

Further Reading

Job Application Handbook, Judith Johnston, How to Books.

Winning CVs for First-time Job Hunters, Kathleen Houston, Trotman Publishing.

Winning Interviews for First-time Job Hunters, Kathleen Houston, Trotman Publishing.